Being Happy
Being Married

Being Happy Being Married

Keeping Love in Your Marriage

LEE SCHNEBLY, M.Ed.

FISHER
BOOKS™

Many of the designations used by manufacturers and sellers to distinguish their products are claimed as trademarks. Where those designations appear in this book, and Fisher Books was aware of a trademark claim, the designations have been printed in initial capital letters.

ISBN 1-55561-322-5

A CIP record for this book is available from the Library of Congress.

Fisher Books is a member of the Perseus Books Group.
Find us on the World Wide Web at http://www.fisherbooks.com
Fisher Books' titles are available at special discounts for bulk purchases in the United States by corporations, institutions, and other organizations. For more information, please contact the Special Markets Department at the Perseus Books Group, 11 Cambridge Center, Cambridge, MA 02142, or call (617) 252-5298.

Text design by Tonya Hahn.
Set in 11-point Janson by Perseus Publishing Services.

First printing, May 2001

1 2 3 4 5 6 7 8 9 10—04 03 02 01

Contents

To all the people who started out as my clients and ended up as my friends.

I'm Beginning to See the Light

I don't know how to change a tire.

I learned English, math, and history in school, and my mother taught me to cook and sew. At church I learned about God, and a piano teacher taught me how to play. But in the giant universal School of Life, I must have been absent on tire-changing day. That hole in my self-sufficiency crosses my mind each time I strike out on my own to drive to another city. I always decide to learn how to change a tire as soon as my trip is over. It's obviously not a huge priority in my life because I still haven't done it. I will only when the motivation is strong enough.

Like most people, I enjoy learning a new skill, whether it's something I need to know or something that's fun. (Some subjects are both.) The process of learning is available to everyone, regardless of age, health, sex, intelligence, or financial status. That means if there's something you don't know, it's only because you haven't learned it yet.

But I still haven't learned to change a tire.

Fortunately I know a mechanic who's willing to trade car maintenance for counseling. But he and I laughingly admit we feel frustrated by each other's refusal to act on our good advice. I keep telling him he's got to communicate more with his wife. He keeps telling me I've got to change my oil more often. Both of us are typical in our responses to good advice. We ignore it.

Another area in which I sadly lack knowledge is finance. I have a great deal of admiration for friends whose conversation is peppered with comparisons of balanced mutual funds, brokered CDs, and index options. For me, managing to balance the checkbook is cause for unbounded joy. Recently a kindhearted friend lent me a giant book on investments. I'm so intimidated by it I haven't gotten past the table of contents. Knowing something about cars and finance would enhance my life because, I believe, dependency diminishes the quality of life. The happiest people are the most self-sufficient.

> The happiest people are the most self-sufficient.

But the fact is, I'm lazy. I don't want to work very hard for the information I lack. I want information that's presented in an easy-to-read, lighthearted way. I want to be able to read it on my patio while I sip iced tea. My favorite history lesson was reading *Gone With the Wind*. As far as I'm concerned, being educated should be gentle and entertaining.

That's why I'm writing this book.

This book is not meant to replace your counselor, if you have one. In fact, good counselors are similar to good mechanics. You need a counselor to help you figure out the problems you've been unable to solve yourself. Most people have the innate capacity for improving their life quite dramatically when they have a little information to help them. It's just that most of us were never taught these skills in school or any place else.

Not knowing how to fix a flat tire doesn't mean I'm dumb. It's something I never learned. The only difference between my fiscally sound friends and me is their willingness to learn the subject. I'll know I've arrived when I can hop out of my car, whip out the spare tire, and confidently exchange it with the flat while I commiserate with my companion about municipal-bond funds!

Skills are skills. Your ability to can peaches or play golf is like my ability to help people get over a depression. They're processes we've learned. Isn't it wonderful each of us can learn almost any skill we want? We can learn many skills simply by reading about them.

I hope you'll enjoy reading this book. It's not a textbook because textbook writing is not a skill I ever wanted to acquire. But it is a helpful book.

If you were to come into my office for counseling, we would deal with your problems in the way I describe here. First I'd ask you to tell me about your problems. I'd jot down a few notes describing what you'd like different in your life. How is life not "working" for you? Who are the people you're having difficulty dealing with? How does their behavior make you feel? What have you tried? What have been the results? How would your life be different if you didn't have these problems?

If I were your counselor, I'd spend our first session getting as much information as I could about your problems. Then I'd have a good grasp of what you want to see changed. In the beginning, I'd be 90 percent responsible for the work because I have to ask questions and formulate ideas that might help you. Your 10 percent would be to express yourself and your feelings.

As we continued in the counseling process, the percentage of responsibility would shift. I would continue teaching concepts, ideas, and skills. You would continue learning them. Eventually you would be 90 percent responsible for the changes you want to make. My responsibility would shrink to only 10 percent as I listen, encourage, and make minor suggestions. Ultimately, you would be 100 percent responsible for your life decisions, behavior, and consequential happiness or unhappiness.

Sometimes I meet a former client in the grocery store and he gives me a hug and says, "You helped me so much!" I accept only 5 percent of the credit. Conversely, I take only 5 percent of the blame if the person is still unhappy. I can be the teacher of skills, but the client himself uses them or rejects them. So he deserves the lion's share of pride as he sees his life improve. Without his efforts, his life wouldn't change one bit.

The purpose of marriage counseling, of course, is to help two people find ways to enjoy one another. It's twice as complex as helping just one. Most often, both parties are disappointed in the relationship, often with one foot in the divorce process.

We all know the best time to seek professional help is early, just as with physical disease. Cancer today can often be cured if it's

The purpose of marriage counseling, of course, is to help two people find ways to enjoy one another.

discovered and treated early in its progress. The longer we wait, the poorer our chances of complete recovery.

The same is true in marriage, but generally one or both parties think "things" will work out. Often they do, but many times they just get pushed deeper and deeper under the skin until they become an enormous and dangerous infection. The job of any therapist is to provide "antibiotics" to help heal the wounds. At the same time, we teach both individuals how to avoid getting infected again.

For physical health, we all know to keep our bodies clean, to exercise, eat a variety of healthy foods, enjoy a minimum of unhealthy foods, drink plenty of water, and so on. For marriage health, maybe we're *not* so sure what we need to do. So the counselor recommends those practices, such as spending time together in conversation, preferably alone, showing affection to each other, sharing some activities, and treating one another with respect.

We also teach what to avoid: disrespect, dishonesty, any kind of abuse, silence, and distancing, to name a few.

Sometimes when a person calls me for information about marriage therapy, he or she may say, "Thank you. My husband and I are trying to decide whether we need it or not. We'll keep talking about it and I'll call you back."

I often suggest they check this book out of the library or, better still, buy one to keep and reread. Any bookstore can order it if they're out of stock. Just reading it can frequently help you spot the causes of your sagging spirits as well as learn how to understand and address the short circuits in your relationship.

In essence you can start to become your own marriage counselors. Reading it together will make it even more effective. It's lighthearted, encouraging, down to earth, and almost certain to help you with the problems you're experiencing. Enjoy the process!

1

We've Only Just Begun

I love weddings. Each one we're invited to gives me weeks of
pleasant anticipation. When the day finally arrives, I like to get
there early enough to get a good seat. I want to relish the sight of
each bridesmaid proceeding up the aisle to music that implies
something important. I delight in watching the ushers walk
purposefully front and center. The groom stands watching for the
first sight of his beloved. And when the bride herself appears in all
her splendor, I can hardly stand it! Inevitably my throat closes and I
struggle to choke back tears of emotion as I watch father and
daughter march bravely and proudly toward the groom.

As I watch the pageant, I puzzle over my overwhelming
emotional response. Maybe these tears are the same kind that can
well up at a parade when the band is playing something powerfully
majestic, with flags being raised by proud young scouts and excited
majorettes flashing batons with practiced skill. The mood is positive,
full of hope and promise. It's the ideal of what we like to expect: Life
is good and people are participating in a splendid ceremony
symbolizing the good that is to follow.

In a wedding, the same elements of pomp and ceremony
entertain us, and in addition we get to re-experience the dream of
how love should be. We all know how love *should* be. Watching a

wedding is kind of like watching a marvelous preview of the coming lifetime of love and happiness.

Surely this bride and groom, as ecstatic as they look, can continue living their lives in this cloud of love. Look at the expressions on their young faces as they repeat the vows! Just hear the earnestness in their voices as they say, "I do." They really mean it!

Those of us watching may reflect on our own marriages. Sometimes we determine again to make happen the promises we made at our own weddings.

At the same time, there are likely to be a few cynics in the congregation. But even their skepticism is the result of having been disappointed in dreams of perfect love. And there are also a few observers (usually the very young) who buy the whole package hook, line, and sinker, with never a doubt that the newlyweds will live happily ever after.

But probably the most emotion wells up in those of us who fall between those two categories. We're neither ardent believers nor cynical nonbelievers. We want to believe in the joyful future of these two people, but we're a little afraid to. We did once, and we've been burned.

We want to warn this couple so they can avoid getting hurt. We want to say, "Wait, dear young people! You're so young and so inexperienced and so vulnerable . . . what you're doing today is such an enormous step you can't possibly comprehend it! We're talking *for life*, here. Commitment of the most mammoth proportions! See, there are so many things you don't realize. It's going to be so much hard work!"

In spite of the hard work that lies ahead for them, we do want them to marry. We see the love and admiration on their faces, and we want them to have the experience of joy that marriage can provide. We want them to know the delight of sleeping in on Sunday mornings and reading the paper together over cinnamon rolls and coffee. We want them to have each other available to listen to stories of what they endured during the day. They can enjoy life so much more fully with a mate beside them who really knows and understands them. They might even get to share the birth of a child and the bonding joy that experience can bring. Even the nights walking a colicky baby should be shared, as should the pride of seeing that baby graduate from high school.

What a wonderful opportunity they have, we think. We might even want to say, "Look, you two. Appreciate this! This can be the start of something so wonderful that nothing else in life can compare. You can make this work! It's a challenge, but you can conquer it if you do the right things. It's all in your hands."

> But deep down inside we wonder if they could possibly know what they just said when they said, "I do."

Maybe it's all these thoughts and feelings welling up inside us that can't help but cause a tear or two. Maybe our own projection of old dreams, hurts, joys, disillusionments, and hopes whirl with such intensity in our heads that we can't possibly separate the good from the bad.

But the bride and groom rarely have such doubts. They are able to say, "I do," with such sincerity and such naiveté that we happily give them our blessings. We want nothing but the best for them as we stand in the reception line waiting to give them both a hug, toast them, share their cake, give them gifts, and watch them drive away to a new life full of promise and expectation.

But deep down inside we wonder if they could possibly know what they just said when they said, "I do." Certainly they meant it, but did they comprehend it? I believe no one comprehends it at that stage in life.

To begin with, two people who have fallen in love are in no condition to make any kind of important decision. They can barely function on any level, so out of their heads in love are they. Rational? Logical? No way. Completely helpless is more like it.

Scientists have studied people in love, trying to pinpoint the physical manifestations the love bug brings. They have found there are actual chemical changes that affect us in many ways.

Most of these are positive. We bloom. We look and feel better than we have in the past. We get by with a minimum of food and sleep, and yet we feel like we could move mountains. The behavior we exhibit is often manic. Euphoric. Excited. We're totally optimistic and ready to tackle anything. So heady are these feelings that falling in love renders us emotionally unstable.

We might almost be labeled temporarily insane. And it's in that wacky, unstable state of near insanity that we make perhaps the biggest decision in our lives—to marry.

Is there any hope for a marriage that was made by two people in that atmosphere? Absolutely.

Then why are there so many unhappily married people?

Because nobody ever taught us how to be married. All we had to learn from was watching the way our parents did it, and usually we determined *not* to do it their way!

This book will provide some ideas about how to be married that may be different from some you've tried. I believe they'll help make your marriage better. If I practice what I preach, they'll make *mine* better as well!

I Do Because . . .

Each of you will need a separate sheet of paper for this exercise. Without discussing it (or peeking!) write down your reasons for getting married. Then, write down what your expectations for marriage were before the wedding (for your partner and for yourself). Compare notes.

2

Through the Years

I want to make a confession here and now: Mine is not a perfect marriage.

Some people may assume that marriage counselors have the process down to a perfected skill, but alas, 'tis not so. Priests, ministers, and rabbis are still known to sin occasionally. Physicians get sick. Models gain weight and get zits. Bridges designed by brilliant engineers have been known to crack or collapse. All of those happenings are a normal part of life.

Don't believe I have achieved perfection in marriage, because it simply is not true. It's not even possible. Though I'd like to be able to blame my husband ("I could have a perfect marriage if he'd just shape up"), I must confess to making a sizeable contribution to an imperfect relationship myself. Not deliberately, but the result is still the same: disappointment on both sides.

Occasionally someone tells me, "We have a marvelous marriage. We've never fought or argued in twenty years." I always smile and say, "How nice for you!" Inwardly I suspect there are flies in the ointment that both people have chosen to pretend don't exist.

Perhaps there are a few good souls who were blessed with mates who match or complement their own personalities. But if even *near* perfection prevails, it's a rare and glorious happening.

> *Don't believe I have achieved perfection in marriage, because it simply is not true. It's not even possible.*

Most of us have to work very, very, very hard to keep a relationship rewarding to both parties.

I know that people sometimes think Larry's and my marriage is one of those made-in-heaven love nests, because we usually look relatively content. In a way it's almost too bad that most of us do walk around looking content, because we perpetuate the myth that we've got it all together. That makes the rest of us feel sorry for ourselves because we know "our marriage isn't as good as most people's."

Larry and I will no doubt continue looking like Mr. and Mrs. Perfect for social occasions, but I want to publicly announce that we don't always act like that at home. There have been times when we've argued all the way to a party, argued as we went up the walk and rang the doorbell, and as the host opened the door, we both beamed merrily and sang a happy "Hi!" We looked calm and pleasant all during cocktails and dinner, actually did enjoy ourselves, said warm thanks and good-byes to our host and hostess, and resumed hostilities on our way back to the car.

I believe that is typical. It doesn't happen to us too often, thank goodness, but often enough to keep me humble as a marriage counselor. About the time I get too big for my britches and think I've got all the answers, we reach another major glitch in our relationship. There is more stress and pain and anxiety while we work through still another difference of opinion.

It no longer frightens me, however. It's kind of like the flu. Now and then you get it. You feel feverish and rotten and discouraged and helpless, but if you hang in there and take good care of yourself, you recover sooner or later. You would never *want* it, but it's a part of life that seems to be unavoidable.

When I feel miffed and vexed with Larry, I can accept the bad feelings the way I do a sore throat. It doesn't signal danger, but it does demand attention. Just like a cold, a marriage needs special care when it's sick.

Many times that fact in itself irritates us. We don't *want* to have to deal with a sick marriage; we just want it to stay well. Of course it would stay well if we took good care of it in the first place, but we usually neglect it.

> We don't *want* to have to deal with a sick marriage; we just want it to stay well.

Perhaps we have to suffer discomfort in order to learn. Certainly, I grew up hearing my mother say that vegetables are good for us, sweets aren't, and so on and so forth. As soon as I hit junior high I rejected most of her advice and stuffed myself with candy bars and doughnuts after breakfasting on fudge and cola. Of course I got fat and pimply and miserable and hated myself. You'd think I would have changed my eating habits immediately, wouldn't you? But instead I continued trying to beat the system for many years, wanting to eat all the things I craved, but avoid the consequences. Now, in my late sixties, it seems so simple. It just isn't worth the price to eat sweet things and feel the sugar highs that turn to lows. Drinking wine makes me dopey, so why do it? I eat giant salads that Mama would have been thrilled to see, and I've come to love them.

All of that gives me continued hope about marriage. I grasp the fact that if I want a blissful state, I have to do something to achieve it. You can't beat the system. A "happily-ever-after" marriage will never just *happen*.

Marriage Is Work

Marriage is probably the biggest challenge we face in life. In my opinion it needs more thought, care, attention, and energy than most other jobs we take on. "Jobs?" Even as I type the word, something in me feels jarred. "Jobs" sounds suspiciously like work.

Am I putting marriage in the same category as cleaning the bathroom? Taking out the trash? Putting in an eight-hour day at the stock market? Building a house?

Yep. And perhaps that reveals part of the problem. Most of us went into marriage with the expectation that it would be the fun that followed the hard work; not more hard work in itself. We're twice as disillusioned when we must come to terms with a state of life that is no longer much fun at all.

But I don't want to imply that marriage is only as rewarding as taking out the trash. I truly believe it can be the most rewarding occupation in the whole world. Marriage must be considered a responsibility that requires consistent attention if it's going to fly. It can and should be fun in the process.

After all, there are jobs and there are *jobs*. I can't pretend I'd love spending eight hours a day cooking hamburgers, but would I love being activities director on a cruise ship? You bet! Would it be fun to be a movie star and work with Harrison Ford? Oh yes!

Probably even cruise-ship personnel find their jobs tiresome from time to time. Having to work up enthusiasm for touring Puerto Vallarta would get to be a drag after you've done it enough times, as would all the other details of being responsible for other people's happiness.

Could it be that I'd even tire of doing love scenes with Harrison Ford? Now *that* I doubt, but I know I'd hate having to get up at four in the morning to do it. Friends who work as extras in the movies at Old Tucson Studios complain of endless boring hours waiting in the 110-degree sun. We who don't make our living that way can't comprehend the trials connected with film-making that make it hard work.

Nevertheless, many people in the business enjoy it. Work can be joyful. You just know that it won't be all fun, and you prepare your expectations accordingly. I would hope that even if I had to cook hamburgers all day, I could find some fun in it while I worked toward goals that would land me a job I'd like better.

The process of work gives us a sense of self-worth. Alfred Adler used to say, "Work is worth." To have nothing to work at would be demeaning and destructive to one's self-image.

Which means that acknowledging marriage as work isn't necessarily unpleasant. Once we recognize it as a task-oriented process, we can tackle it with enthusiasm and make it satisfy us in so many ways.

Marriage Is a Choice

Is it for everyone?

Not in a million years. Some people should avoid it like the plague. Folks who put a high priority on independence and autonomy might never be willing to pay the price of constantly working together. Many of us should also avoid taking jobs as cruise-ship directors or movie stars, because we're not temperamentally suited for people-involved positions. We might make better architects, engineers, artists, computer analysts, or composers—fields that don't demand a lot of interpersonal relating. That doesn't make us faulty or lacking or wrong. In fact, it indicates we have the wisdom to know ourselves, to know what we like and don't like, what we're good at and not so good at.

Society has made marriage almost a given for so long that lots of people choose it because they think it's expected of them. They know no other way. That is becoming less true today, as we see more people living single than ever before. I think it's marvelous that we're coming to see marriage as an option rather than a necessity. Perhaps it's a necessity only if we want to have children, and some people even disagree with me on that score.

It's too bad that we can't figure all this out long before we reach the age of marrying, because it might prevent some of us from jumping into a way of life that is totally inappropriate. But given the "insanity" that overtakes us when we fall in love, we often couldn't make a wise, well-thought-out decision if we tried.

> Society has made marriage almost a given for so long that lots of people choose it because they think it's expected of them.

Marriage Isn't a Fairy Tale

So let's say we're married. We got married way back when we were young and foolish (or old and foolish) and thought it was going to be great, marvelous fun living with this perfect mate.

Job Interview

If you looked at your marriage as a career choice, what would be your job description? What would be your spouse's job description? In the space below, write out these descriptions for yourself and each other.

Wife

My job description: _____

_____

_____

_____

My husband's job description: _____

_____

_____

_____

Husband

My job description: _____

_____

_____

_____

My wife's job description: _____

_____

_____

_____

Now we're disillusioned. It's anything but fun. It's a drag. We're both disappointed and discouraged. The starry-eyed expectations have turned into a living hell. Can this be how marriage is supposed to be? Do other married couples feel this low down? Surely not. If I am married and so unhappy, I must have an unhappy marriage, right?

Not necessarily. In fact, *probably* not. In most cases it's a matter of mistaken beliefs and expectations that didn't materialize. Most of the time the relationship can be vastly improved. That is the purpose of this book.

I meant it when I said that if I practice what I preach, it will help even my marriage. Much of the time there's nothing wrong with an institution or a process; it's just that the people involved are doing it incorrectly. I find that immensely encouraging. I can change my behavior if it's going to make me happier.

I was heartened a few weeks ago when I confided to our son Lyle, "Dad and I are having problems again," and heard his response. Lyle (thirty-six and married at the time) said confidently, "As long as you guys keep trying, it'll be okay. Just don't quit trying, that's all."

I saw the confidence in his eyes and gave him an appreciative hug. He's right, of course. (How did this little kid get so smart?!)

It's never going to be *easy* improving our relationship. Larry and I are different in so many ways, it's downright remarkable we get along at all! I know he suffers as much as I do from time to time.

But both of us are committed to our relationship and we'll keep hanging in there until we improve things. With two people constantly changing and growing—frequently in opposite directions—it's an enormous challenge to keep readjusting the dynamics of living together.

I'm always the one saying, "We've got a problem. We need to talk." He rolls his eyes and looks to the heavens pleadingly as if to say, "Not again, Lord. Make her stop."

But I am relentless. I never stop, at least not for long. And I know he doesn't really want me to stop, because if we ever stop, the marriage is doomed. We want this marriage.

When Larry and I met almost fifty years ago, I wouldn't have dreamed that our marriage would ever require any work. We were madly in love; our song was "Tenderly"; our future would surely be nothing but bliss. Now I'm older and wiser. I know there are times when our marriage needs work.

3

Daydream
Believer

If I had to identify the biggest cause of marital unhappiness, I'd say it's the set of expectations we have about marriage in the first place. In most cases, each of us has had some twenty to thirty years to formulate our beliefs as to what marriage should be like, and we think we know what to expect when we finally make the commitment. Whether we want to emulate the relationship we saw between our parents or completely avoid interaction like theirs, we have definite ideas about how marriage should be.

Here is where we get in trouble. It would be different if we went shopping for a spouse the way we shop for a car. We have definite likes and dislikes. And most of us take a lot of time searching for the one car that comes closest to fulfilling all our wishes.

We consider price, appearance, mileage, brands, and optional equipment. Regardless of our budget, we usually shop carefully. If we buy from the classified ads, we interview the seller and take the car to our trusted mechanic for a checkup. If we buy from a dealer, we consider his reputation as well as that of the manufacturer.

When I bought my last car, I knew exactly what features I wanted and how much I could spend. I stood firm on all the items I wanted, shopping at several dealers until I found the one that had what I could afford in a car that met most of my requirements. Even then I questioned the salesman at length about warranties and service. By the time I drove the car home, I knew precisely what I was getting and what kind of performance I could expect. We'd signed a contract with everything down in black and white. It had been an interaction based on logical communication, facts, figures, and legalities.

Marriage? It's just about as opposite as can be.

Oh, there are some similarities, to be sure. In both cars and spouses, we have firm ideas as to what we want and how we expect them to perform for us. But that is where the similarities end.

In choosing mates, we let our emotions, rather than facts and logic, guide us. We don't make a considered decision. We fall in love when we least expect it.

> "Now I believe in love at first sight."
>
> "When he came into the restaurant, I said to another waitress, 'There's my future husband.' "
>
> "The first time I met her, I was turned off completely, but the second time I knew she was the one I wanted to grow old with."
>
> "My kids loved her, and I knew she'd be a good mother to them."
>
> "It was during the war. I was to ship out the next week, so we eloped after knowing each other for just two weeks."
>
> "He reminded me of Brad Pitt."

It's fun to hear our reasons for deciding to marry. Granted, a few people take plenty of time to decide, but most of us don't take nearly enough time. We willingly and eagerly jump feet first into a lifelong commitment without ever thinking, *buyer beware*. The only warranty we get is, "Till death do us part."

Would anyone in his right mind buy a car like that?

Imagine seeing a car with a "For Sale" sign in its window and deciding that *that* is the car we'll drive for the rest of our lives because it's such a neat shade of blue. Although it's a ridiculous thought, it isn't unlike many of our reasons for marrying.

But let's say we're smarter than the average person. We've taken a lot of time to think about our needs in marriage. We've "shopped around" for years and gotten to know what the opposite sex is all about. We've dated dozens; we've rejected and been rejected. We've become so wise and discerning we can spot the potential problems in a relationship within the first couple of dates.

We willingly and eagerly jump feet first into a lifelong commitment without ever thinking, *buyer beware*. The only warranty we get is, "Till death do us part."

And one day we meet Mr. or Ms. Perfect. Warily we begin to let ourselves think, "Maybe this time . . . "

We agree on total honesty. We talk endlessly and discover more and more similarities. We come from the same socioeconomic backgrounds. Our spiritual beliefs are compatible. We laugh a lot and enjoy the same activities. We both want or don't want children. We even agree on wanting to live in the same city forever. Our families like each other. The physical attraction between us is nothing short of fireworks and Disneyland. Wow, this is *it* . . . this is really *it*! We've been together for a year and now we're sure. What a marriage this will be!

We tell everyone how perfectly matched we are. "We think alike about *everything*!" we rave. "We have the same standards, beliefs and values."

"Well, there are going to be problems," people might warn, to which we say quite happily, "Oh, sure! Of course there will be problems. We know *that*! But we're so good at communicating, we'll work them out. You'll see."

Underscoring the confidence in our relationship skills is the knowledge that we're IN LOVE. Love conquers all, everybody knows that. Problems? Piece of cake!

And it's true that with love all problems can be solved. Actually, they can be solved even *without* love, when there is enough communication and mutual respect.

But one of the biggest potential problems is often built into the marriage from the start. Most of us enter into marriage with an unspoken contract, so to speak, and most of us assume that our spouse-to-be has the same contract in his or her mind.

Contract

1. I hereby agree to give you all the power in my life.
2. I renounce the right to make myself happy, knowing that from now on you will do it for me.
3. I will look to you for all my companionship, instead of having additional friends in my life.
4. Every need I now have, I expect you to fill.
5. In exchange, I will try to fill your every need. This gives me the right to advise and control you, because I know what is best for you.
6. With our responsibility for each other, we must match each other's moods. If you are angry, I will be angry, too. I'll be sad when you are sad, and expect sadness when I am sad. If one of us worries, the other must also worry. One must never be happy unless both are happy, no matter how long it takes—if ever.
7. Because you are the most important person in my life, should I ever be unhappy, it will clearly be your fault; it is therefore your responsibility to try to reverse my mood.
8. Our signatures on this contract negate any responsibility for our individual selves that we might previously have held.

Signed:

_____ and _____

There you have it, and I'm reasonably sure none of us would have signed it had it been presented to us before the wedding. Yet, foolish as those statements are, many of us expected marriage to make us happy.

Notice that in most of the statements, one gives up responsibility and hands it over to one's mate. Granted, that would be a wonderful luxury, if it worked. Think how glorious it would be to have someone whose purpose in life is to make you happy, whatever that might take!

A fringe benefit would be the permission to blame all one's troubles on one's mate. "If I'm married and I'm unhappy, I must have an unhappy marriage, and it's your fault. You're supposed to make me happy. It says so in the contract we signed."

You'll never hear anyone say those words because they sound so obviously unfair, and yet many of us unconsciously hold beliefs like those.

Power

The first statement in the contract, "I hereby agree to give you all the power in my life," is clearly unthinkable. Oh, sometimes it can be a handy cop-out: "Gee, I'd love to come with you to your fitness center, but my husband won't let me go out at night."

But if the husband really won't let the wife go out at night, I would predict trouble down the road for that couple. When one person rules another, it is not a mutually respectful relationship, and the submissive one is almost sure to rebel somewhere along the way.

One possible exception is a traditional religious marriage, in which wives willingly agree to let their husbands make the rules. I do know some happy couples who subscribe to that decision, but it works only when both people keep their part of the bargain. I'll address that issue in a later chapter (see page 215).

Most of us are comfortable living in relationships based on equality, but that takes enormous amounts of decision-making and discussion of needs and wants. We may want equal rights and equal responsibility but be unwilling to spend the time it takes to work out such an arrangement.

> We may want equal rights and equal responsibility but be unwilling to spend the time it takes to work out such an arrangement.

But you can't have it both ways. If you want to share the load equally, you must accept the idea of continuing conversation, compromise, negotiation, and respectful communication for the life of the marriage.

On the other hand, if you want to have all the power, you have to take responsibility for making your partner happy. If you want to be the one without responsibility, you need to give up your autonomy and learn to enjoy the freedom that comes from making no decisions. It's all a trade-off.

Only You Can Make Me Happy

If you did choose to give your mate all the power in your life (although I certainly don't recommend it), you could then state the second belief on the contract: "I renounce the right to make myself happy, knowing that from now on you will do it for me."

I know men and women who seem to have that expectation. They appear to be totally lost if the other person gets involved in activities that exclude them. It's as if marriage became their only source of happiness and their mate the only provider of it. Ooh, what a horrible concept! I shudder to think how miserable I'd be if all my happiness depended on Larry, or his on me. Thank goodness for all the opportunities we have to make *ourselves* happy, whether married or unmarried. We can make ourselves happy at any given hour of the day or night.

Granted, sometimes it's a challenge. If I have stomach flu and I'm throwing up at two in the morning, it's nearly impossible to make myself happy. But it's just as impossible for Larry to make me happy in those circumstances. Meanwhile, I can always choose a nice book to read while I rest between trips to the bathroom.

But many of us complain profusely if this part of the "contract" is broken. I admit I've done it a million times myself: "Larry loves sports so much he's never there to do things with me." Sniff. Even so, I'm confident that if we were asked to agree to this statement before the wedding, we would probably decline the offer.

"Whitney, will you marry me?"

"Sure, Jason. As long as I no longer have to make myself happy. You will do that for me, won't you?"

The sad thing is, Jason might even agree. And both he and Whitney will believe it! That is the price of being in love—we think we can do anything.

Actually I've found people to be consistently happy or unhappy regardless of whether they're married or single. People either know how to enjoy life or they don't. Getting married doesn't alter that fact. Getting old doesn't either. Old, young, married, or single, we decide to make ourselves happy or unhappy. One thing I know for sure: No one else can do it for us.

I have heard people blame their problems entirely on their mates. Mothers of unhappy adults sometimes say, "You know, Kathy was happy when she lived at home with her family. She was always laughing and carefree until she married Phil. He's got to be the cause of her problems."

Though that might seem to make sense, it's more likely that Kathy was happy at home because her family spoiled her. Parents who try to make their children's lives completely happy might be depriving them of the opportunity to grow and develop self-reliance. Regardless of whom those children marry, they may never be able to find a mate who treats them as dotingly as good old Mom and Dad did.

It may be that Kathy will leave Phil only to find that nobody else "makes her happy," either. She needs to develop her own resources if she is ever to be happy—or else live the rest of her life with Mom and Dad to nurture her.

> People either know how to enjoy life or they don't. Getting married doesn't alter that fact.

In any case, I wouldn't agree to that part of the contract if I were you. God forbid you should ever find yourself entirely responsible for someone else's happiness!

My Only Friend

Let's go on to the third statement, "I will look to you for all my companionship, instead of having additional friends in my life."

More women than men seem to make this mistake, although I see both sexes do it. We *should* be each other's best friend when we marry, but never each other's *only* friend.

For one thing, we can't think like the members of the opposite sex. Hard as I try, I can't imagine what goes on in men's minds. Obviously, they can't comprehend my thoughts and feelings, either, or we wouldn't have the misunderstandings we do. Many men understand other men easily, just as many women understand other women. Remember Professor Higgins in *My Fair Lady* singing, "Why can't a woman be more like a man?"

Listen to a group of women at a party commiserating about men. You'll generally hear at least one say, "I can't believe he didn't know how I felt." I can. Men rarely know quite how women feel. But all the women will nod with understanding and share their stories of disappointment in men's behavior.

> We *should* be each other's best friend when we marry, but never each other's *only* friend.

Now listen to a group of men at the same party. Will their conversation be the same? No way. They'll be talking about sports, politics, or their jobs. We women *wish* they'd discuss us, but in truth they're tickled to death to have people around them who don't even want to talk about feelings and relationships.

So we need friends of our own sex. Each of my women friends fills a different role in my life. With some I talk about our kids and our houses. Some always like discussing men. A few like to dig into things like feminism or politics. Some are soft, others tougher. Some are genuinely interested in what I have to say. Others talk nonstop but are very entertaining. Although I treasure them all, I'd hate to be on a desert island with only one friend.

Now, I happen to believe that we should have friends of the opposite sex as well, but a lot of folks disagree with me. I maintain we can stay faithful to a mate and still enjoy other men and women as friends.

Unfortunately, the number of extramarital affairs around us does seem to lend credibility to those who say, "No, we can't. Look at him and her and her and him; all cheating on their spouses."

I can't deny it happens. But not with me. And not with the vast number of people who make the decision to stay faithful and do exactly that. If I ever cheated, I'd have to eat my words, admit I erred, and give up my men friends. That thought alone will keep me faithful!

I say anyone can stay faithful and still enjoy friends of the opposite sex. I must emphasize, however, that openness and honesty are essential when we have friends of both sexes. I have to be able to say, "Frank and I had lunch" as naturally and openly as I say, "Virginia and I had lunch." The minute I start withholding the fact that I'm having lunch with Frank is the minute I'm heading for trouble.

So? Cancel out number three in the contract. I'll look to others for companionship as well as to you, my dear. Aren't you glad?

Take Care of Me

What about statement number four, "Every need I have, I expect you to fill"? Dumb, huh? But I know women who pumped their own gas when they were single and now expect their husband to do it for them. "It's a man's job to take care of cars. Why haven't you changed my oil?"

There is certainly nothing wrong with a division of labor. If a man doesn't mind taking over the car care and a woman doesn't mind taking over the laundry, that is great. That is simply cooperation. (If they both want to keep up their survival skills, they could trade every three months.) But when dependency rears its ugly head and men "can't" cook and women "can't" pull up weeds or do income-tax forms, they both lose something.

When dependency rears its ugly head and men "can't" cook and women "can't" pull up weeds or do income-tax forms, they both lose something.

It's better to say, "Every need I have that I can possibly fill, I'll continue to fill. I'd appreciate it if you would do the same. But I'm also open to negotiation and sharing certain responsibilities."

I Know What's Best for You

The corollary to the above is statement number five, "In exchange I will try to fill *your* every need. This gives me the right to advise and control you, because I know what is best for you."

This trap is awfully easy to fall into, especially for many women. We tend to be good caretakers and nurturers and, when acting out of love, we become motherly to our husbands if we're not careful. To fix a sumptuous dinner is a loving thing to do, but insisting he eat the vegetables is overstepping.

Many women have an amazing ability to notice people's needs and wishes. A woman at the dinner table usually sees when someone is looking for the salt and provides it right away. But that same trait can mean that a woman notices everything and becomes a sort of guardian.

"Honey, I don't think you should wear that jacket; it's too big," I told Larry one night.

"I love this jacket," he said contentedly and left the house wearing it proudly.

I bit my tongue and disapproved.

Next time he put it on, I managed a loving smile and a sugary voice as I said, "Sweetie, that jacket is so big, it makes you look awful."

He gave me a quick kiss, smiled, and zipped up the jacket.

Each time he wore it, I would roll my eyes, giggle, or make snide remarks. Even as I did it, I knew it wasn't my business. Maybe it was all right the first time I mentioned it. But when he assured me he liked the jacket anyway, I should have accepted that. What makes me think I know best? I don't know, but I confess I sure do think that a lot of the time.

I can give Larry good advice about everything from what to eat to how to do his job. There is nothing I don't know! And I'll delightedly share it even if he does not want the benefit of my wisdom. In case he didn't hear me the first time (or the thirty-first), I'll repeat it in different ways. I might even mention it to the kids, hoping they'll mention it to him.

In my defense (of which there is precious little), I think that bad habit has its roots in loving and caring. "I love you so much, I'll help you every way I can. Now, do things the way I tell you. It's for your own good, of course. Whatever would you do without me?"

This habit can make people crazy. It isn't reserved only for women; men do it, too. Often these people are excellent executives or workers who have a great deal of control over others. They *think* that way: "What does this company need to increase efficiency?" And then they go home and give instructions to dust first and vacuum second rather than the other way around. Huge arguments result! "Look, I'm only trying to make your job easier. Vacuuming first doesn't get the dust you brush onto the floor when you dust first. Don't you *see*?" (I actually had a couple in counseling who belabored that point for half a session.)

The point is, it doesn't matter. My friend George says, "It's practically impossible to overestimate the unimportance of almost anything."

> It's practically impossible to overestimate the unimportance of almost anything.

He's right. Let's show our love by letting people decide for themselves what to wear, what to eat, how to clean, and so on. It's so much more respectful than believing they need our advice.

Matching Moods

The next point in the contract addresses feelings and behavior based on emotions. It's surprising how suggestible we are to other people's moods. Let one bummed-out person be grim and grouchy long enough and hard enough, and the entire family, office, or classroom may very well follow suit. It seems almost contagious to have someone around exhibiting strong feelings. If that's true in a work setting, it's even more true at home.

We seem to wholeheartedly believe that "With our responsibility for each other, we must match each other's moods."

Perhaps it seems we're showing respect for another's crankiness when we act cranky, too. I am aware of a certain reluctance to sing and dance for joy in the same room where someone is darkly angry. But isn't it foolish? I wonder why we feel we must tiptoe around a person who is at odds with his world. Maybe we're afraid of appearing unsympathetic.

But at least it's something we can ponder and discuss with those we care about. We could ask them if they want us to match their moods. I'm guessing most of them would say, "Of course not." Given that permission, then, would we be willing and able to act however we feel? Or would we continue to be quiet and withdrawn when our mates are? We can only try it and find out.

The agreement, "If you are angry, I will be angry, too," may depend on who is the object of your anger. If you're angry at a coworker or a neighbor, I'll be glad to join in and play "Ain't it awful?" with you. We can both badmouth the jerk and have a marvelous drama in which we agree (for once). It is fun to have a common enemy at times. We can give it our all for ten minutes and then put it aside and do something different.

But if it's *me* you're angry with, that is a horse of another color. No way will I join you in being angry at *me!* Instead, I'll probably get very angry at you for being angry at me. And we can play out that scene for a lot longer than ten minutes. How about all evening? Maybe even all week. You want anger, you got it, Buster.

See, I have to do that in order to punish you for your anger. My private logic says that if I punish you enough, you'll start acting as I want you to act—loving me dearly at all times and never getting upset with me. Most of us are pros at manipulating people with our emotions.

My friend and colleague John Daley maintains that any time we're angry for longer than ten minutes, we're trying to manipulate a person or a situation.

When I first heard him say that, I was dubious. But I've checked it out many times and now agree with him. If I bump my head on a cupboard door, I may feel a surge of anger for . . . what, maybe a minute or two? Not for long, because there is no one to manipulate. I won't stay mad at a cupboard door, and I certainly don't want to stay mad at myself. So I quit being angry.

But if you do or say something that hurts me, I can stay angry at you for a long, long time. I probably won't even be aware that I'm trying to "whip you into shape" by making you uncomfortable.

> Any time we're angry for longer than ten minutes, we're trying to manipulate a person or a situation.

Anger does beget anger. We'll talk more about that later. All we need to do now is decide whether we choose to continue being angry just because someone else is.

The same is true for the remaining statements, too, about matching sadness with sadness and worry with worry, and not being happy until the other one is. It's all part of the unconscious belief that we should feel the same at all times.

Though it may be difficult not to get dragged down when another person is, we can give ourselves and each other permission to work at improving the ability. Will the upset person think we're unsympathetic? Possibly, if they've been used to getting sympathy in the form of a glum face that matches their own. But once we establish our insight and motives, those around us can begin getting used to this new, better way to live.

Remember the old song, "It All Depends on You"?—"I can be happy/I can be sad/I can be good/I can be bad/it all depends on you."

What a hell-on-earth existence that would be, and yet many of us allow ourselves to wind up in that situation. We need to see that we've put ourselves there, recognize how foolish it is, and quit doing it.

You Are Responsible for
My Feelings

The next statement in the contract says, "Because you are the most important person in my life, should I ever be unhappy, it will clearly be your fault; and it is, therefore, your responsibility to try to reverse my mood."

Notice that word "try."

Did you every try to make someone happy who is determined to stay unhappy? Most of us have. Most of us have been in the opposite position, too, fiercely hanging on to our unhappiness while someone tries to cheer us up. There is almost a triumphant ecstasy in staying miserable just to defeat them!

How marvelous to be able to blame you for all my behavior! We all enjoy having someone to blame. In fact, I have a good friend named Eric who volunteers to be this someone. He's got an unparalleled sense of humor and is virtually unflappable, and he says, "Hey, if you want anyone to blame for your problems, you can blame me. I don't care." So I hereby invite you to blame all your woes on good old Eric. He can stand it!

We won't do that, of course, because that would end the game playing we so enjoy with our mates. If I'm angry at Larry for inviting a dinner guest without checking with me first, I don't want to blame Eric. Nor do I want to forget the incident. I certainly don't want to forgive Larry or he might do it again.

No, I have only one course of action: Blame him long enough and hard enough so he will never again even *consider* doing anything like that. I've got to teach him a lesson he won't soon forget.

Now, of course, I wouldn't deliberately and consciously think those thoughts, because that would make me a mean, controlling, self-centered shrew. I won't disclose my feelings or my goals. I'll just be cool and withdrawn. Larry will figure it out sooner or later.

If I really want to solve the issue in a respectful way, I might say something like this: "Honey, when you bring home an unexpected guest for dinner, I feel really embarrassed because I look like death and also because all we have in the house is that Eggplant Surprise that nobody would eat. I need your help to find a solution."

That opens the way for respectful negotiation, which is far more likely to solve the problem.

Time to Renegotiate

Well, that about wraps up the contract. It is tempting to sign something that promises, "Our signatures negate any responsibility for our individual selves that we might previously have held." Zowie! Freedom from responsibility! What a heady thought.

It reminds me of the time in third grade when Sister Mary Domitilla told the class that if any of us ever gave someone else permission to sin, we would have that sin on our souls. The class Rotten Kid, Jimmy, raised his hand and asked, "Sister, if somebody tells me I can do something bad, then does that mean I get off scot-free?"

Sister assured him firmly that it meant *both* people would be guilty of the same sin.

Well, heck. If giving somebody else the responsibility for my life isn't going to get me off scot-free, then maybe I won't sign the contract. Not just yet, anyway. Let's finish the book and think about it.

What Are *Your* Terms?

Discuss each point in the contract on page 16 with your spouse. How many of these points have you been *acting* as if you believe, even if you wouldn't put it in those words? Try to think of some examples of when each of you acted on any part of this contract.

Now, in the following pages, draw up a new contract. For example, instead of the first point, you might say, "I hereby agree that we do not need to control each other or ask each other's permission to lead our lives as we wish, but we will recognize when our decisions affect each other and make every effort to communicate our needs and wants honestly."

Old Contract: 1. I hereby agree to give you all the power in my life.

New Contract: 1. _____

_____

_____

_____

Old Contract: 2. I renounce the right to make myself happy, knowing that from now on you will do it for me.

New Contract: 2. _____

_____

_____

_____

Old Contract: 3. I will look to you for all my companionship, instead of having additional friends in my life.

New Contract: 3. _____

_____

_____

_____

Old Contract: 4. Every need I now have, I expect you to fill.

New Contract: 4. _____

_____

_____

_____

Old Contract: 5. In exchange, I will try to fill your every need. This gives me the right to advise and control you, because I know what is best for you.

New Contract: 5. _____

_____

_____

_____

Old Contract: 6. With our responsibility for each other, we must match each other's moods. If you are angry, I will be angry, too. I'll be sad when you are sad, and expect sadness when I am sad. If one of us worries, the other must also worry. One must never be happy unless both are happy, no matter how long it takes—if ever.

New Contract: 6. _____

_____

_____

_____

Old Contract: 7. Because you are the most important person in my life, should I ever be unhappy, it will clearly be your fault; it is therefore your responsibility to try to reverse my mood.

New Contract: 7. _____

_____

_____

_____

continues

Old Contract: 8. Our signatures on this contract negate any responsibility for our individual selves that we might previously have held.

New Contract: 8. _____

_____

_____

_____

Signed:

_____ and _____

4

Two Different Worlds

One of the first questions I intend to ask God when I get to heaven is why women and men are so different. The longer I live, the more amazed I am that the sexes manage to get along at all! We deserve medals.

It's no wonder both sexes are fraught with disappointment and frustration. We think that because we're all human beings, there must be some similarity in our thought processes. In truth, we might do just as well trying to communicate with creatures from other planets.

Men and women don't think alike, let alone speak the same language. Our needs are vastly different, as are our expectations. When we say the words "I do," we're foolish enough to believe we're both agreeing to the same principles. Maybe those words should be changed to "I wish" or "I want." Or "I will if you will." We should stick in a bunch of "unlesses" and "except whens."

But if we rewrote the marriage ceremony, defining attitudes, expectations, and gender differences, we'd have three hundred pages with lots of "whereas . . ." phrases. It would be a hopelessly complicated legal process that would stop any of us from attempting it.

So it's just as well we stick with the simplistic format we have, because it allows us in our naiveté to enter marriage with confidence, unwarranted though it may be.

All we really need to change is our belief that men and women are reasonably alike. Instead, we have to accept the truth—that the rare occasions on which we see things with the same perspective are only happy accidents.

> All we really need to change is our belief that men and women are reasonably alike.

Before I continue, though, I want you to know that I realize how often generalizing gets us into trouble. Sure as a person says something like, "Southerners are always gentle and sweet," someone else is going to say, "Ha! If you knew my husband's aunt Sallie Mae, you wouldn't make that ridiculous statement. Those Southern women are hard as nails!"

If one says, "First children in a family are always perfectionists," another is going to pipe up, "Yeah? My uncle Joe's been in prison for twenty years for forgery. Guess he's not as perfect as everybody thought, huh?"

To say, "Men want sex more often than women do," is sure to strike a chord in some women who challenge that with an irate, "*My* husband hasn't been a decent lover in twenty years. *I'm* the one who wants sex."

Just about any generalization is arguable, so please forgive me for using some. I generalize only to demonstrate how the sexes differ, and, admittedly, we don't all differ in the socially common directions.

That being said, I'll continue with the most common differences I see between men and women, knowing that in all examples, the persons could be reversed.

The Devil Is in the Details

For one thing, women tend to think in great detail. We grasp millions of trivialities in any one experience, engrave them indelibly on our photographic memories, and assume men do the same thing.

Men, on the other hand, think way more broadly, in global terms, dismissing the trivialities as unimportant.

Why do we entertain the idea, then, that a couple can easily communicate with pleasure for any great length of time?

Here is a couple going home from a dinner party.

She: Mark is the best cook in town. The way he heated the brie just ever so slightly and then topped it with a sauce that was sweet but with some horseradish to make it zingy! Wasn't that good?!

He: Good food!

She: He does everything like that. He must have had a million classes in gourmet cooking. There was mint in the vegetables, too. I noticed that their friends from Nevada were pretty miffed with each other, did you?

He: Who?

She: The couple from Nevada.

He: Who were they?

She: They sat right across from us. She was wearing a turquoise cotton top and a white skirt and lots of Indian jewelry; and he had on a denim shirt and Levis. Did you notice his watch? Indian made. It had the biggest obsidian stones I've ever seen. It was magnificent, wasn't it?

He: Oh, the guy who used to be a Marine?

She: I don't know what he did. I just could see that he and his wife were hostile. Did you notice how she never laughed at his jokes?

He: He was a marine. He was telling us about the war. Fascinating stuff.

She: But I wonder why they were so mad at each other. When everyone clinked glasses during the toast, they avoided each other's.

He: We talked politics. He's a strong Republican.

She: He sure drinks a lot. He had three scotch and sodas before dinner, about five glasses of wine during dinner, and two brandies after.

He: (silent)

She: Did you notice?

He: Notice what?

She: How much he drank. I thought he'd fall asleep at the table, he looked so snockered.

He: (long silence)

She: So, what else did you guys talk about?

He: Oh, I don't know . . . the World Series, who might go to the Superbowl, the greenhouse effect.

Somehow the conversation doesn't seem to jibe. And when they're en route to another dinner party six months later, it will go like this.

She: I wonder if the Nevada couple will be there again tonight.

He: Who?

She: The couple from Nevada, remember? She wore the turquoise cotton top and all the Indian jewelry; he wore denim and Levis and a watch with big obsidian stones; and they were hostile. Remember? They avoided each other all evening; didn't even clink glasses during the toast; she never laughed at his jokes; and he was a Marine, you said.

He: Hmm. I do remember an ex-Marine, I think. I'm sure looking forward to watching the game after dinner.

And we wonder why men and women have problems in so many areas. The way they perceive life touches every facet of their marriage. Like birthdays. She will remember that he likes smoked almonds, and she'll buy him some and present them elegantly wrapped, along with a shirt of a color he doesn't have, two ties that accent it perfectly, monogrammed stationery, and his favorite aftershave.

Furthermore, she will have enjoyed the process of shopping for just the right card, wrapping each gift in different paper, and fixing a sumptuous dinner with a birthday cake and candles. She's good at all of those things.

The catch is, she expects her birthday to be remembered with the same care and thoughtfulness. I can't tell you how many tearful wives I see within a week after their birthdays.

"My birthday was Wednesday. I thought for sure he'd buy me one of the things I'd said I wanted. I talked about at least ten things I wanted in the worst way. He could have bought any of them, and I would have been thrilled. But no, he did nothing about it. I waited all day. I thought maybe I'd get flowers delivered—I had balloons sent to his office for his birthday. But no . . . no flowers, no card. That night I hardly spoke to him. He finally realized. He raced out and bought flowers and a card at the supermarket and said I should go pick out something special as a gift from him the next day. Well, let me tell you, I didn't, and I won't. I can't believe how insensitive he was. And after all I did for him on his birthday!"

It's basically a difference in the sexes. He flat doesn't remember details. But he can learn to, if he realizes the importance of it.

Teaching Each Other

I recommend that wives begin talking about it a month before their birthday. Put up a wish list on the refrigerator and talk about it often, adding gifts you'd like from time to time. Define the perfect birthday. Tell him where you'd like to eat out, if you want him to get a sitter, if you want to include the kids in the celebration, and so on and so forth.

"But that takes all the fun out of it," wives protest. "I want him to think of it! I want spontaneity and surprise!"

"You can have all that someday," I reassure them, "but you have to do the teaching now. In just a few years he'll know what to expect, and you won't be so disappointed."

Children need to be taught how to dust furniture, how to wash dishes, how to do things the way we want them done. Employees in new jobs require training, and employers expect to teach. People of all ages take classes to learn skills they didn't previously have.

Wives need teaching as well. We don't know what irritations our husbands will feel at some of our seemingly normal behavior. When Larry and I were newlyweds, I was getting out some records (yes, we called them "records" in those days and played them on things called "phonographs" or "record players"), but I wasn't as aware of the need to keep them clean as Larry was.

I remember the tone of horror as he said, "No! You're getting salami on Frank Sinatra!"

> We expect each other to think and act the same as we do. All we need is the open-mindedness to teach each other what we'd like.

Then he taught me always to hold records by the edges, never putting fingers on the grooves. I hadn't known they were that delicate, but I didn't mind doing what he demonstrated.

He also said he'd been embarrassed that I'd left some crumbs on the butter when we visited his parents' home. This mattered to him, and I haven't left a crumb anywhere since!

So it is with any relationship, only we rarely stop and think about it. We expect each other to think and act the same as we do. All we need is the open-mindedness to teach each other what we'd like.

It's hard, though, for men to act the way women want them to because they often don't feel the way women want them to. They can't. There are innate differences in men and women besides the obvious physical ones.

Accept the Things You Cannot Change

Gary Smalley, a minister and psychologist, explained to a women's group I attended: "Little boy and little girl babies are identical at first. At conception they're both little girls. But early on in the pregnancy the boys get a big bath of testosterone and that changes them dramatically. In fact," he twinkled, "it destroys a part of their brain, the part that thinks and feels like little girls think and feel."

The women all tittered, of course, and reveled in the thought that "we're dealing with brain-damaged people here. That explains a lot!"

I think the good fellow was an expert at wrapping the audience around his finger, but I suspect what he was getting at was that there are true physical differences in the brains of men and women.

You can't get a cow to think like a lion. I believe women are more disappointed in men than vice versa, because women's minds expect a lot more attention to detail than is comfortable for men's minds.

Women seem able to think of six different things at the same time. A woman can carry on a phone conversation while she chops celery for the soup, fixes peanut-butter sandwiches for the kids, and motions them in to eat while she's letting in the paperboy and getting out the checkbook, writing him a check, wiping the kids' faces and sending them off to play . . . all the time planning what to fix for dinner.

If a man is on the phone and his wife whispers loudly, "Tell Jack we'll bring back the hedge trimmer tomorrow," the man usually looks confused, shakes his head to indicate he doesn't understand, and continues talking. She repeats the message, uses body language to demonstrate hedge trimmers and says loudly, "We'll return it tomorrow," but he continues looking totally blank. Finally he says with some annoyance, "Just a minute, Jack," sets down the phone and asks, "What is it?" Only then can he comprehend the message.

I know that is not true of every man, and to you men out there who are bristling at unfair generalizations, I apologize. I know better than to believe all generalizations, and I realize there are many men who can run circles around women when it comes to carrying on six different thought processes at the same time.

I recognize, too, that women may be accusing me of old sexist stereotyping. They're thinking, "She's got us chopping celery and doing kitchen things like women did in the forties. Doesn't she know there are women like me who are CEOs? I'm president of a corporation. I do things besides wipe peanut butter off my kids' faces!"

Yes, and I'll bet those chief executives are doing six things at once from their polished oak desks in their penthouse offices overlooking the city. They can apply their detail ability to whatever setting they are in.

But my point is this: Women think along several tracks at the same time. Men focus on one or two until they finish, then turn their attention to one or two more. That can be a plus. They're putting a more concerted effort on one task, spending the major part of their energy on solving that one problem before they attack another. They are often less fragmented than women and more goal-oriented. Often their endurance level is far superior to women's.

When I see TV clips of men working to put out forest fires, for example, I'm mightily impressed with their tenacity. They appear before the cameras looking exhausted, unshaven, discouraged, but relentless in their battle and dedicated to their goal. The same with rescue teams, for a mine tragedy or a missing child. Men go willingly to meet the need and continue unceasingly until the job is done. Everything in them is focused on that one need. I'm glad they have that ability because I certainly don't.

I like men's strength. I admire their selfless tenacity and dedication to doing a job well. But I want them to think more like women, to be more conversational, more into feelings.

I don't think we can have it both ways. But that does not stop us from wishing we could. That is where the pain comes from: Our expectations are disappointed too often.

Enjoy the Differences

My daughter Lisa said one day, "Maybe we're looking to men for something they don't have to give. It's like picking up a dog and trying to iron with it. You'd say, 'Darn it, this dog isn't getting the wrinkles out.' You can't blame the dog for not being an iron." Sounds sensible to me.

Maybe we need to be more appreciative of the qualities that make us different rather than wishing the opposite sex were more like us. Ideally we would complement each other, each having strengths the other lacks.

Men can make terrific playmates! Most men are eager participants in anything that smacks of fun, and we women don't take enough advantage of that. They're always delighted with an adventure, whether it's a game in which they compete or one where they watch others compete. They'll even indulge in a food fight if you will. They have so much "little boy" still inside them that they can help us be more childlike and open to playing, if we let them.

Usually we won't. We're so busy being sensible that we don't have time to play. Women always "need to talk." We're a pretty serious lot, we women, wanting to straighten out all our problems "if it takes all night."

I think it's good that at least one of us will be a driving force to keep communication going, but we should have fun as well.

Interestingly, much of the playing children do is already indicative of the differences in sexes: the very sounds they make, for instance, as they're learning to talk. There was a study that showed baby boys make noises most of the time when they're experimenting with talking. Meaningless noises, but in great variety. Baby girls try to say words and string them together in sentences even before they can actually talk.

Our grandson Christopher began shooting with imaginary guns when he was barely two and didn't even own a toy gun. He would break off part of a cracker and aim at trees and make shooting sounds.

At the same age, the little girl across the street was lovingly holding her baby doll.

> It's very difficult to change the pictures in our minds that define "how men act" and "what women do."

Who We're *Supposed* to Be

In addition to the innate sexual differences, of course, men and women are separated by the roles that have been taught us for hundreds of years. It's very difficult to change the pictures in our minds that define "how men act" and "what women do."

One of the major differences is how we deal with anger. Men are generally comfortable expressing their feelings in a confrontational way. In a work setting, a man can release anger audibly and forcefully to his employees and colleagues, and he's respected for his aggressiveness.

Women, on the other hand, are called "bitchy" if they have the audacity to be as vehemently vocal.

Dr. Harriet Lerner described it very well in her book *The Dance of Anger*:

> Women have long been discouraged from the awareness and forthright expression of anger. Sugar and spice are the

ingredients from which we are made. We are the nurturers, the soothers, the peacemakers and the steadiers of rocked boats. It is our job to please, protect, and placate the world. We may hold relationships in place as if our lives depended on it.

Women who openly express anger at men are especially suspect. Even when society is sympathetic to our goals of equality, we all know that "those angry women" turn everybody off. Unlike our male heroes, who fight and even die for what they believe in, women may be condemned for waging a bloodless and humane revolution for their own rights. The direct expression of anger, especially at men, makes us unladylike, unfeminine, unmaternal, sexually un-attractive, or, more recently, "strident." Even our language condemns such women as "shrews," "witches," "bitches," "hags," "nags," "man-haters," and "castrators." They are unloving and unlovable. They are devoid of femininity. Certainly you do not wish to become one of them. It is an interesting sidelight that our language—created and codi-fied by men—does not have one unflattering term to de-scribe men who vent their anger at women. Even such epi-thets as "bastard" and "son of a bitch" do not condemn the man but place the blame on a woman—his mother!

Dr. Lerner's book is one of my favorites and I often recommend it to men and women.

It's difficult to know just how much of our difference in attitude and behavior is innate and physiological and how much is unconsciously learned from role models we observed. The line that separates the two will no doubt always be fuzzy, but we can agree that the sexes act and think and feel very differently from one another.

Some of the differences will diminish as society gets better at equality. Some never will, though, because we're not created the same in the womb.

And that is good.

When it comes right down to it, we seem not to want to be married to people who are exactly like us. I know a few men who think more like I do than Larry does. But the attraction is not there for me. Men to whom I gravitate have different personalities from mine.

A toddler boy these days is generally not given toy guns to play with. His parents do their part to discourage violence in any form. What they usually find is the little guy biting off bits of his graham cracker, like our grandson, to form the shape of a gun, which he points at his parents delightedly and says, "Bang! Bang! I shot you!"

The toddler girl across the street is hugging her baby doll, dragging around in her mother's high-heeled pumps, and wearing a long string of pearls as she serves pretend tea to her Teddy bears.

Some years down the road, the little boy will put aside his cracker guns and fall in love with the little girl. They will assume that they think and feel exactly the same about everything, and they'll marry without a qualm.

It will take them both a while to discover how differently they feel about almost everything.

Getting to Know You

Obviously, neither of you will fit neatly into a male or female stereotype, so how do you go about discerning your unique differences and what is truly important to each of you? Of course, talking to each other is the easy answer, but sometimes we're so used to the way we see things, we don't even think to talk about everything we really need to know. Some things seem too trivial to discuss until an incident shows us it was perhaps not so trivial to both parties.

Following is a list of general interest questions and incomplete thoughts. Start by going through the list together, taking turns answering the questions and completing the thoughts. Be careful to allow the other person to answer uninterrupted—you may be surprised by your spouse's answer to questions you assumed you knew!

1. My favorite time of day:

_____

2. I would describe myself as the color _____ because

_____

3. Something I wish all people would do or be:

_____

4. I feel productive when

_____

5. My ideal vacation:

_____

_____

6. A perfect party would be like this:

_____

_____

7. My favorite kind of music:

_____

8. I feel like the fairy tale character _____ because

_____

9. The holiday with the most meaning for me is _____
because _____

_____

10. Three things I'd like to be doing in three years:
    1. _____
    2. _____
    3. _____

11. When I'm in a large group,

_____

_____

_____

_____

12. Something I like to do that seems out of the ordinary:

_____

13. A special gift I received when I was a child:

_____

14. My mother would describe me as

_____

15. Bragging is

_____

16. Competition is

_____

17. Spontaneity is

_____

18. TV influences my life in these ways:

_____

_____

19. My favorite childhood game and why I liked it:

_____

_____

20. If I had six extra hours in the day,

_____

21. My best year in school:

_____

22. If I could spend a whole day with my best friend,

_____

_____

23. A scary dream I had:

_____

_____

24. My favorite movie star:

_____

continues

25. A compliment I recently received:

_____

26. I would describe myself as the musical instrument
_____because_____

_____

27. Three reasons I like myself:
    1. _____
    2. _____
    3. _____

28. Honesty means

_____

29. Hitchhiking is

_____

30. Space travel is

_____

31. The pet I would most like to own:

_____

32. My favorite TV show:

_____

33. Music affects my life in the following ways:

_____

34. My father would describe me as

_____

35. When I want to avoid doing something, I

_____

36. My favorite sport and why I like it:

_____

37. I am the kind of person who

_____

38. My favorite childhood story was _____ because

_____

39. A family tradition I enjoy:

_____

40. The greatest dessert in the world:

_____

41. I decide between right and wrong by

_____

42. Surprise parties are

_____

43. As a child, bedtime was

_____

44. The last time I lost my temper:

_____

45. The kind of house I would most like to own:

_____

46. On my next birthday, I would like to get

_____

47. The worst job I ever had to do:

_____

48. One time when I was teased,

_____

49. One time when I was lost,

_____

50. One of my secret desires:

5

Games People Play

Any of you who are parents and any of you who *had* parents know that parents teach their children many skills that will help them fit in and be happy and successful in society.

Most skills are taught and labeled clearly:

"Christopher, this is how you dig with a shovel. See? Take the shovel like this, put the dirt here. Now you can stick this little plant in the hole. Let's water it and watch it grow. That's how you garden. Christopher is going to be a good little gardener!"

"Christopher, our friends are coming over for brunch today. When they hold out their hands, like this, you shake hands with them, like this. Give them a nice smile and say 'How do you do?' "

"Ack, Christopher, no, no, no! Don't unroll the whole roll of foil!"

"I *liked* the way you hung up your jammies, Christopher. It's good to be neat."

That's called *parenting*.

Every child ever born got more parenting than he or she would have liked and learned vast amounts of useful information before ever starting school. The process is never-ending. Parents love to teach their children.

But there is one social skill we parents teach without ever mentioning it. We would never ever give it a name. It must be done subtly. Still, even though we don't define it, we teach it more certainly than we teach gardening techniques. We model it daily, sometimes even constantly.

By the time the child is five, he's almost as good at it as his parents. He understands it, can do it himself, knows when other people are doing it and how he should respond, but he hasn't the foggiest idea of its name.

He may hear it defined for the first time in his twenties or thirties and suddenly realize that he can do that! Or, more likely, he realizes that someone around him does that. Over the years he becomes more aware of the universality of the skill. In his forties and fifties, he's incredulous at its continued use and proven power.

What is this skill?

Manipulation.

A Family Tradition

It permeates the atmosphere, affecting every relationship. Not only do mothers and fathers use it, so do children, teachers, lovers, executives, and workers in every capacity. It's like the air around us, ever-present, and we take it for granted as we do air. It's what is.

Among *Webster's* definitions of manipulation are these: "To treat or manage with the intellect. To control the action of, by management; to manage artfully or fraudulently."

Gracious. We wouldn't want to teach *that* to our children any more than we would lying, stealing, or cheating. But teach it we do, expertly, thoroughly, unceasingly, and in exactly the same ways our parents taught it to us: by giving frequent demonstrations. We may have fine-tuned the manipulative skills we learned from our parents and refined them into a masterful art that we hand down to our babies as soon as possible.

Why do we do that? Because manipulation works! Whatever works is something we want to use and

> We get rid of something only if it *doesn't* work. Manipulation is so effective that it will probably be kept in our families for generations, maybe forever.

keep and polish. We get rid of something only if it *doesn't* work. Manipulation is so effective that it will probably be kept in our families for generations, maybe forever.

Are there any better ways to get our needs met? Of course there are, but am I willing to give up the old tried-and-true skill of manipulation? Gee, I doubt it. I've used it for so long that I'm afraid I'd miss it if it weren't around.

Act One: Lessons from Mom

Imagine the scene if manipulation *were* taught like other lessons are taught.

> Mother might pick up her toddler, hug and kiss her and say, "Baby, today I'm going to teach you something wonderful! You're going to love it. It's something you can do whenever there is something you want and it looks like you're not going to get it. It's called *manipulation*. Can you say that word?"
>
> "Ma-nip-a-shun?" Baby lisps.
>
> **Mommy:** Very good! Now this is what it means. Say you want a new game at the toy store in the mall. You ask Daddy for it and he says no. You really want that game, so you coax him a little. But he still says you can't have it. Now here comes the good part. You ma-nip-u-late Daddy. You look very, very sad and you walk slowly. Make sure you keep looking down at your feet. Don't say a word, now.
>
> Sooner or later Daddy will notice that you're looking at your feet, walking ever so slowly and not talking and he'll say, "What's wrong, Baby?"
>
> Now I know you'll want to tell him, but you mustn't tell him yet. You sigh first. Can you sigh? Like this. Good! Good girl! You make your voice very, very soft and you say kind of pitifully, "Nothing, Daddy."
>
> **Baby:** But something is. I want my game.
>
> **Mommy:** I know, dear, but you have to do it this way, because this way works. Trust Mommy. Mommy *knows*. You keep walking more and more slowly, looking sadder and sadder. Never ever look right at Daddy, you understand?

Always look away from him. When you get to the car and
he's fastening your seatbelt, start to cry quietly. He'll ask
again what's wrong.

Baby: Can I tell him now?

Mommy: No, not yet. Be patient. Sometimes it takes a
long time. You ask him for a tissue to wipe your eyes and
you keep crying, looking sad and looking away from him.
Now, it may not work right away, Baby. You may have to
look sad and sigh a lot for a few more days before Daddy
will go back and get you the game. But don't look at him,
whatever you do. Except at bedtime when he kisses you
good night. Then look right into his eyes and say, "I love
you, Daddy," and hug him very tight. Then turn away and
sigh a big, loud sigh.

Baby: Like this? (sigh-h-h-h)

Mommy: Perfect! Oh, Baby, Mommy's so proud of you!
You're going to be a good little manipulator like Mommy
is! Now, you watch me a lot and you'll see more and more
how easy it is to do. In fact, tonight at dinner I'm going to
ask Daddy to paint the kitchen. Watch carefully and see
Mommy manipulate!

End of lesson. And I can imagine you male readers feeling a kind
of vengeful, "A-ha! I *knew* it was a carefully thought-out system." But
men, too, are masters of the art. Let's peek at another scenario.

Act Two: Lessons from Dad

Dad: C'mon, Sport, Dad's gonna teach you a new game.

Sport: Oh, boy, like soccer?

Dad: No, this one doesn't take a ball or anything like
that. This is a game that helps you get whatever you want.

Sport: *Anything*, Daddy?

Dad: Anything. And it helps you get out of doing things
you don't want to do, too. Let's say Mom wants you to

clean your room and you don't want to. You can't just refuse; you'd get in trouble. You learn to manipulate.

Sport: Oh, boy!

Dad: See, women can't stand it when men get mad at them. That's your best bet when you don't want to do something—get mad at them. First you put it off as long as you can; that's called *procrastinating*. But when you finally have to buckle down and clean the room, make sure you look real mad. Throw things around in there. Slam a couple of drawers. You can even say some bad words if you want. When you're done—and by the way, don't do a good job; that's real important—come out looking like a thundercloud, you know what I mean?

Sport: You mean like you looked when Mom asked you to transplant the rosebush? Is that like a thundercloud?

Dad: Right on, Sport. You got it! Ha, ha, you're gonna be a great thundercloud, kid. You're my kid! And don't speak to her. If you have to say anything at all, glare at her. Before long she'll quit asking you to do anything. She'll do it herself because she won't want to see you glaring at her.

Sport: How long do I have to glare and not speak to her, Dad?

Dad: Ah, good question. Keep it up all day for sure, and maybe even the next day or two. Except if you're talking to someone else. Say, if your buddy comes over, it's okay to talk and laugh and have fun. Just act like Mom isn't even there. But when he leaves, make sure you get real quiet again. Someday when you have a wife you'll have this thing down to a science. It's how men have to treat women. I used to see my dad do that to my mom. Just act mad and quit talking when they bug you about *anything*. Eventually they quit bugging. Now, keep your eye out and watch me the next time she asks me to do something.

Act Three: Finale

Let's go on to the scene when Mommy asks Daddy to paint the kitchen. Both children's eyes are wide as they watch the drama unfold.

> **Mom:** Honey, how about another cup of coffee? I got the mandarin-chocolate blend you like so much and ground the beans myself. Was it a good day? You certainly looked nice this morning when you left. I was proud of you. You look so much younger than our friends' husbands.
>
> **Dad:** Yeah? Thanks! (grins broadly) Sure, I'll have another cup. It's great.
>
> **Mom:** I've been wanting to have your boss and his wife over for dinner.
>
> **Dad:** That would be fine. Say when and I'll mention it to him.
>
> **Mom:** The only thing that's holding me back is how awful this kitchen looks.
>
> **Dad:** Looks fine to me. What's wrong with it?
>
> **Mom:** Oh, honey, it's terrible! It's needed painting for two years now.
>
> **Dad:** Yeah, well, it's not bad, really.
>
> **Mom:** Not bad! I couldn't possibly have people in when the house looks like *this*. Especially your boss.
>
> **Dad:** Then don't have them. Or don't let 'em in the kitchen (laughs). Hey, it's time for *Frasier*.
>
> **Mom:** But, honey, let's decide about the kitchen.
>
> **Dad:** What's to decide? I don't have time to paint, if that's what you mean.
>
> **Mom:** Sigh-h-h-h. (Baby's eyes widen with interest.) I just want to help you have the kind of image that will impress your boss. I try so hard to help you. Maybe I can paint it myself (sigh-h-h). I could get up early in the mornings, like at four o'clock or so, so I could get in a couple hours of painting before I iron your shirts and buy groceries for you to eat.

Dad: For me to eat? Don't you eat? Can't I have any peace around here, for God's sake? It's nag, nag, nag the minute I come through the door. You think I don't work hard enough all day that I feel like coming home and working hard here, too? You don't want a husband. You want a slave you can boss around!

Dad exits angrily and turns on the TV while Sport watches eagerly.

Mom cleans up the kitchen quietly, blowing her nose from time to time. Later she joins the family in the living room and talks to the children, but avoids looking at Dad. The children have just seen the lesson of manipulation acted out before their very eyes.

To complete the demonstration, both parents continue modeling their prescribed behavior for days. They go about their roles with practiced ease, playing their parts with magnificent timing and expertise.

Eventually Dad paints the kitchen, making sure to splash paint on almost every surface. He glares and glowers except when his buddy stops by and they take a few hours off to watch a game. He finishes the paint job in stony silence, icily ignoring any attempts Mom makes toward friendliness, and he continues that behavior for an additional week.

Baby is learning that Mom's techniques did indeed get the kitchen painted. Sport observes how men operate in order to avoid being controlled. We can be sure that by the time they're ready to marry, they will have developed the same expertise and timing as Mom and Dad.

A No-Win Situation

The problem with manipulation is that while both partners are experts at their crafts, they won't necessarily be playing the same game. When we try to manipulate each other, it's like I'm playing Monopoly and you're playing Chinese checkers.

Both of us are playing our very best, and we're master players, but somehow it isn't working. We both *know* it isn't, and we're

> When we try to manipulate each other, it's like I'm playing Monopoly and you're playing Chinese checkers.

pretty sure the other person is playing "wrong." We try harder to make this game work, and we try to win, but it won't ever resolve because I'm using paper money and plastic houses while you're using marbles and dice.

We watch each other play and we feel increased frustration at the seeming hopelessness of the whole experience. We know the rules, but why doesn't the other person follow them?

The wife who says, "He should come ask me what's wrong when I'm crying in the bedroom," can't imagine herself failing to ask that of anyone crying anywhere.

The husband says, "The thing that turns me off more than anything else is when she cries. I refuse to get involved when she pulls that."

His game plan is "If I ignore her behavior long enough and hard enough, she'll quit that crying nonsense."

Hers is "If I cry long enough and hard enough, he's bound to feel sorry for me."

And there are ten thousand variations for every game. Those who grow up in the same family know all the rules and variations that were "taught" in their home, but even they are likely to have made different decisions on how to beat the system.

This person never cries. He just sighs and looks sad. That one yells and screams. She quits speaking. He glowers. She gets drunk. He eats too much. She quits eating entirely. He develops a nervous stomach. These two cry constantly; those two argue to win but never to resolve an issue. He acts martyred. She has an affair. He tries to dominate and control. She goes limp and passive. He lies. She confronts. She denies. He accuses. She packs a suitcase and moves out. He romances.

And one of the funniest things is this: At some level, both people enjoy the whole process. Give it up? Change? Never!

I still remember the couple who yelled fiercely at each other, even shouting cruel obscenities, while I tried vainly to establish an atmosphere of order and respect in which we could work toward a sensible solution. After a few weeks, the husband stopped cussing at the wife and turned to me. "Are you saying I shouldn't cuss at her?"

"Exactly what I'm saying," I beamed. "Just keep your voice at a respectful level and tell her what you want, how you feel, what you'd like from her."

"Let me ask you something," he said.

"Sure. What?"

"Don't you and your husband yell at each other?"

"No."

"Never?"

"Never."

"How the hell do you stand a boring relationship like that?" he demanded. He and his wife looked at each other in total agreement. A marriage without yelling and screaming was just too dull for them. They left together and never came back.

Changing our patterns of behavior is often an unacceptable option. We don't want to change. We just want the other guy to change. And probably the other guy doesn't want to change, either, even if he's uncomfortable.

Many of those who yell and scream rather like it. Who in his right mind, they wonder, would choose to give it up? The same is true for any kind of manipulative behavior. It's what we learned as children. We're experts at crying, pouting, rebelling, withdrawing, or whatever we've practiced over the years. No way are we going to give it up.

But if we could let go of our unhealthy games, we would be amazed at the amount of time we'd have to enjoy. I often think of how simple life would be if we all agreed that on a certain date, everyone in the world would stop manipulating.

If we could get our needs and wants met without all the emotionalism we've been wasting, wouldn't it be terrific? To solve problems in a forthright, logical, respectful way without the tears and hurt and anger—is it possible?

> We don't want to change. We just want the other guy to change.

You bet.

Then what's stopping us? Nothing.

Would that really improve our marriage? Magically!

So how do we start? Read on.

Model Behavior

Think back to your childhood and, in the space below, write out examples of how your parents demonstrated manipulation. What did they do to make a point or to get what they wanted? Have either of you picked up these behaviors? Or did you learn to behave differently in *response* to these behaviors?

Husband

How my parents demonstrated manipulation:

_____

_____

_____

_____

_____

_____

_____

How I responded (I followed their example, I did the opposite, one parent influenced me more than the other, etc.):

_____

_____

_____

_____

_____

_____

_____

Wife

How my parents demonstrated manipulation:

_____

_____

_____

_____

_____

_____

_____

continues

How I responded (I followed their example, I did the opposite, one parent influenced me more than the other, etc.):

_____

_____

_____

_____

_____

_____

_____

6

R-E-S-P-E-C-T

Needs versus Wants

First of all we must establish the fact that we have few actual *needs*. Most of what we like to call *needs* are really *wants*. Certainly we prefer calling them needs, because that makes them seem essential to our very lives. We might be reluctant to ask for and expect someone to indulge us in whatever we want, but we have no such compunctions against expecting that treatment when our needs are concerned.

So our communication is peppered with the word. "I *need* sex every day," some husbands insist. To which I respond, "No, you don't. You might *want* sex every day, or five times a day, but you would survive very well without it." (They don't believe me.)

Probably our actual needs are only food, water, shelter, and medical care. I'd throw in clothing and love, but I suspect we could survive without even those if we had to.

But life would be grim if all we ever had met were our needs. There is nothing wrong with wanting more, and we have every right to express our feelings, thoughts, and descriptions of what we want out of life. We simply must recognize the difference between those wants and our needs.

Some common "needs" I hear expressed (or express myself) are these:

- I need at least nine hours of sleep.
- I need to have my coffee first thing in the morning.
- I need to know I'm appreciated.
- I need a lot of peace and quiet.
- I need privacy.
- I need people.
- I need excitement.
- I need security.
- I need constant change.
- I need affection.

I don't suppose people will ever change their conversational habits enough to use the word "need" only when it's absolutely true. But if we can recognize the word as slang and not allow ourselves to believe that our wants are needs, life may be a little less frustrating.

The quality of our lives depends a lot on what we want and how we attain it. We have the right to work for what we want as long as we're not hurting someone else in the process. Sometimes we have the right to work for what we want even if we are hurting someone else in the process. It's okay to punch out a thief who's robbing a little old lady, even if it's hurting the thief.

Young adults often enjoy chewing on moral concepts and discussing "truisms" that suddenly seem false to them, and that's good; that's growth. "Is it all right to steal a loaf of bread and give it to a starving child?" Hopefully even we "old" adults still enjoy pondering and discussing ethics and morality, and continuing to develop our beliefs.

All of that, however, explains why needs and wants become so confusing. I might genuinely believe I need something, or at least want it so strongly that I feel I must have it. Larry might believe exactly the opposite.

How in the world can two people with different wants survive together in harmony? Not easily, that's for sure. But certainly they have the capacity to resolve their differences in wants, and even to enjoy the process of resolution. Usually our mistakes lie in not expecting to have to deal with differences. Somehow we manage to convince ourselves that our wants make more sense than the other person's.

The Oughta Wantas

The "oughta wantas" rear their ugly heads, and we complain long and loudly about all the things our mates oughta wanta do, or like, or see, or avoid, or indulge in. "She oughta wanta have sex more often!" "He oughta wanta spend more time with me and the children!"

Our own wants are so strong that we can't imagine the other person's not being the same. We spend a tremendous amount of emotional energy trying to convince our partners that we're right and they're wrong.

Really, we could simplify our lives immeasurably by taking the right and wrong out of most discussions. It's true that some clear-cut behaviors are wrong to almost everybody, and other taboos are culturally or religiously or socially based, but a great many are rooted only in our own unique thinking. ("This is right because I think it is, and you should think that way, too.")

> Our own wants are so strong that we can't imagine the other person's not being the same.

So many fights are fought because of an innate "need" to win. To prove we're right and they're wrong. It's rare that we can change anybody's mind, but that doesn't stop us from trying.

The process of trying to change someone's mind is often actually fun, and I love to play the game with willing partners. My brother, Paul, and I can argue on any subject for hours on end without getting the least bit ruffled. It is a game in which no one has to give up anything or change in any way. Once in a while, he'll convince me of something, and I suspect I've changed his thinking occasionally. But neither of us has an investment in the other one's changing.

That's a very different situation from trying to change our spouse's mind because his or her behavior is affecting our life. When we believe our happiness is being prevented by our mate's actions, we have a strong emotional investment in changing his or her mind. We play to win. We manipulate. We fight dirty. We go for the victory no matter what it costs. Often the issue is power: Who's right?

Competition versus Cooperation

A discouraged wife recounted a battle with her husband: "I am so jealous of his friend. My husband is like a kid with a best buddy, and they want to do everything together, like two little boys. Last night we had made plans to go to a movie together when the phone rang and it was his pal Doug. I felt the hackles rise the minute I heard him say, 'Hey, buddy!' I knew Doug would be wanting him to do something, and I knew my husband would agree to it. I was making all these motions to him, shaking my head, begging him to decline, but sure enough, he agreed to go out with Doug. When he hung up I was furious at him, and guess what he said: 'If I had turned Doug down, you would have won, and I would have resented losing to you.' "

Losing is threatening to most of us, and we often base our decisions on that one point.

In any relationship, we can have competition or cooperation, but never both at the same time. The only exception to that rule is playing team sports, when we cooperate with our team and compete against the other team. But in marriage there is no team—just two individuals cooperating or competing.

When you compete, you can't possibly cooperate. And, of course, the best way to solve problems is through cooperation. When competition rears its ugly head in a love relationship, it temporarily overrides the good feelings of tenderness and affection and revs up the fight-to-win mentality.

I did say "temporarily," however, and the minute we become aware of competition we can withdraw and change our direction. Probably the simplest way to proceed is with self-disclosure: "I just realized I'm competing with you. I don't want to do that. I really want to cooperate and see what we can do to solve this problem. Let me try again."

The Oughta Wanta Exercise

In the space below, each of you write down what your spouse's "oughta wantas" are. For example, he might say, "She thinks I oughta wanta hear all about what her coworkers say to her," and she might say, "He thinks I oughta wanta cook for him because all women are nurturing." If you get stuck, think back to some recurring arguments and try to figure out what assumptions your spouse was making about how you should feel, act, or think.

She thinks I oughta wanta . . .

_____

_____

_____

_____

_____

He thinks I oughta wanta . . .

_____

_____

_____

_____

_____

> *No one* **wins in a marriage war. If one seems to win, the other withdraws only for the purpose of figuring out how to punish the winner.**

Saying words to that effect would be quite disarming to a spouse primed for further battle and would hopefully get the dialogue back to problem-solving instead of war.

War in a marriage solves nothing. It only makes things worse. *No one* wins in a marriage war. If one seems to win, the other withdraws only for the purpose of figuring out how to punish the winner.

Never once have I said sincerely to Larry, "Thank you, my love, for pointing out my faults so completely. I appreciate, too, your guiding me as to what I should be thinking and doing. I shall try my hardest from now on to keep in mind how I might improve!"

Nor has he ever said it to me. What do we do instead? We dip into our bag of punishment tricks. These consist of manipulative behavior we've already found effective, such as distancing, withdrawing, pouting, ignoring, and other common behaviors.

One couple confessed to not speaking to each other for six weeks after an argument! Finally, the husband held a sign around the corner of the kitchen that said, "Do you want to go to a movie?" The wife was ready to laugh and call a truce.

It's a great story, but it seems a lot of work to quit speaking for that long—indeed, for any length of time. The time spent in not speaking is an enormous drain on one's energy, not to mention the total lack of solution it affords.

We might agree to use the time better in noncompetitive conversation that would be useful in at least three ways:

1. We get to express our feelings instead of carrying them around as heavy burdens for who knows how long.
2. You know me better when you hear what's on my mind, and vice versa. You have a constantly updated report on this spouse of yours. You know what I'm about, whether you like it or not.

3. We now have an agenda on the table to attack together.
We know where to focus some energy in order to make
the problem disappear.

Self-Doubt

That all sounds so simple, and even as I write it, I wonder why
Larry and I aren't always able to operate that efficiently. Any two
six-year-olds ought to be able to grasp these concepts and make
them work, right? Wrong. I think I know why.

My self-esteem is not quite up to snuff, and neither is Larry's.
Neither is anyone else's.

Of course, I don't know that for a fact. Perhaps there are a few
blessed souls running around with near-perfect self-esteem, who are
able to say to themselves, "Interesting that this person disapproves
of me so strongly. I hope I can calmly help find the problem so that
we might find a pleasant camaraderie together!"

Most of us go into code blue at the slightest negative comment
and shift into irrational, wild-eyed, nonproductive behavior: tears,
anger, whatever. We feel attacked and unworthwhile when someone
registers any complaint that sounds as though we're to blame. Often
our response has nothing to do with the facts, whether or not we are
to blame. It has to do, instead, with our feelings as we hear the other
person express something negative.

So many, many things go into any one remark a person might
make. Let's pretend I wake up one morning feeling grumpy. I ate at
bedtime, had a restless night, got awakened by a raucous bird
outside my window at dawn, weighed three pounds more than I did
yesterday, and thought again of the enormous pile of ironing waiting
for me after work. I shuffle out to the kitchen and, as I put my bread
in the toaster, I ask Larry, "You have a church meeting tonight?"

Now, granted, I've already established a reputation for
resenting how many activities take up his evenings, but this morning
I'm not looking for a fight. I only want to know his schedule.

He has awakened with a fierce backache from driving all day
long the day before and a bank statement that wouldn't resolve with

the checkbook late last night. He's looking for milk and finding only a tablespoon left in the milk carton. His favorite banana bread is all gone. He hears my question and with lightning speed interprets it as still another attack on his priorities.

"It's here on the calendar," he states a little more loudly than necessary, considering we're standing only two feet apart. "It's been on the calendar for some four months. We meet *every* Tuesday night. This is Tuesday, right?"

"I know what night it is. I only thought that since you met last night, maybe there wouldn't be a meeting tonight." My tone is hardly sweet and tender-loving. And now I cast about for ammunition. "And you have a basketball game tomorrow night, right?"

"Right," he replies with ominous softness. "Is the banana bread all gone?"

"If it isn't there, it must be all gone," I say, implying that any ninny might figure that out.

In short, our morning is off to a rather dismal start. How can that be? We didn't want it to be this way. We're two pretty nice people who have high regard for one another, a lot of respect and caring, not to mention a longer than forty-eight-year marriage. Why are we trading arrows on this lovely morning?

Because of a lot of things. Because of poor sleep, too much work, headaches, backaches, no milk, and no banana bread. That, on top of my sensitivity to his moods and his to mine, gives us the makings of a nice little quarrel.

It doesn't mean we don't love each other. It means we're both experiencing some disappointments in living that are actually relatively unimportant. That's all it means. It has practically nothing to do with our marriage or with each other.

Those same feelings and thoughts, expressed between two people with high self-esteem, might stop at this point. Both might look at the other, laugh, shake their heads, and go about having a wonderful day.

But not so with people who aren't sure they're okay. We're so easily threatened by a perceived criticism that we lose perspective. I find myself wondering, "Does he prefer doing everything with other people? Doesn't he enjoy my company anymore? If I were different, somehow, maybe he'd want to spend more time with me. He knows me better than anyone else in the whole world, so if *he* sees me as faulty, I must be. I should have bought milk. I should have made more banana bread. I should be better in bed. I spent too much time on the kids instead of on him." Behind my terse negative words lies a whole chicken house full of self-doubt and self-blame that, again, have very little to do with Larry or our marriage.

> I suspect we're like a lot of people—unsure of our own value and worth, and, therefore, much too quick to take almost any comment as a reminder of failure.

He is thinking, too. "Am I such a jerk? I try so hard to be a good husband. It's not like I chase women or drink or lie. But she's resentful of me and she used to love me so much. I've fallen short of her expectations. I can't seem to measure up anymore. I should have spent more on her birthday present, maybe. It's because I'm not good at fixing things. I should be better in bed. I wasn't involved enough with the kids. Damn! I just can't do it right."

I suspect we're like a lot of people—unsure of our own value and worth, and, therefore, much too quick to take almost any comment as a reminder of failure.

The crux of the problem, then, is self-doubt. That's what gets in the way of two reasonably intelligent adults being able to discuss and solve problems without pain. Ideally there should be no pain in problem-solving. We have needs and wants. How can we help each other achieve them?

And, in fact, the process is simple in other relationships. When our friend Bill comes to work in the yard, I can say, "Bill, these are my priorities: First trim the pyracantha, then the Texas ranger. The yucca has outgrown its pot; it needs to go in that barrel. Trim the ivy off the ground and rake up pine needles for as much time as you have left, okay?"

Bill might say, "The yucca won't do well in that barrel; it needs full sun."

"Oh. Okay, where shall we move the barrel?"

"How about here?"

"No, that's our route to the garbage cans. Maybe here?"

"That'll work."

"Great. Thanks."

Never once have Bill and I clashed or hurt each other emotionally. We're together for a common cause and we make decisions easily and efficiently. Work gets done, problems get solved. There are no hidden agendas.

Marriage is so loaded with hidden agendas, it's a wonder we survive it at all, let alone with any good grace. We have so many fears and hurts left over from long ago, and they all live in our houses with us and our unsuspecting mates. We spouses often have no idea of the leftover garbage our wives and husbands are still dealing with.

> We have so many fears and hurts left over from long ago, and they all live in our houses with us and our unsuspecting mates.

A very common one is the issue of control.

Control

One of my clients, Ian, is a dear, gentle man. He and Jill were treating themselves to some marriage counseling as their anniversary present, which I thought was a delightful idea for a gift. One issue we dealt with was Ian's anger at almost any request Jill made of him. What emerged was the resentment he still carried toward the control his late father had exercised over him. Dad had been a strong and dominant figure with little praise for Ian—mostly criticism. Ian never could measure up to Dad's expectations, and any work he did under Dad's orders was joyless and tense. He dreaded his father's demands and developed anxiety about demands that carried over long after Dad was dead.

When Jill would ask Ian to do something, he inwardly cringed. No matter how nicely Jill phrased a request, she saw Ian bristle and darken, and his mood become hostile. If he did the job, it was as tense and joyless as if he were minding his father some forty years ago. He didn't understand it, and certainly Jill didn't. No wonder resentment cropped up between them, as any request she made started a cold war.

Ian was responding according to habit, and it was a habit of fear. Fear dictates a lot of negative behavior. So much so that at least one psychologist states that people feel basically only two feelings: love or fear. Gerald Jampolski, in his book *Love Is Letting Go of Fear*, writes that if we're not operating from love, we're operating from fear.

I recommended that book to Ian and Jill to help both of them understand the old fears Ian was struggling with: being dominated and controlled, and feeling helpless and discouraged. Jill needed to see behind the anger and know its roots to deal with it effectively. Anger on her part only reinforced the fear in Ian, and the vicious circle was in motion. Gentleness and encouragement from her would eventually help him relax and learn there was nothing to be afraid of anymore. Previously her response to his anger was distancing herself—withdrawing and becoming preoccupied and chilly, which only reminded him more of his disapproving father.

> When we can understand each other's fears, it's a lot easier to take our mate's bad behavior as a symptom of their inadequacies rather than as an attack on us.

When we can understand each other's fears, it's a lot easier to take our mate's bad behavior as a symptom of their inadequacies rather than as an attack on us. Generally that's all it is.

Sometimes I think we're all like giant stuffed animals wearing ugly Halloween masks. Inside we're soft and cuddly, but we've acquired these masks in our childhood and we put them on to hide behind or scare "bad" people away. They're our defense, and sometimes we're afraid to take them off. Perhaps they serve us in the outside world; perhaps we occasionally need them. But, really, I doubt that they serve us very well in any circumstance, and I know for sure they only hamper us in a marriage.

It's no fun for a Teddy bear to cuddle up to another Teddy bear who's wearing a monster mask.

What's the solution, then?

Turn the page.

7

Have I Told You Lately that I Love You?

Of all the possible solutions that will let two nice, soft Teddy bears get rid of their monster masks and cuddle up to each other, there is only one that really works: communication.

To talk. To converse. To share feelings, fears, anxieties, hopes, dreams, memories, and wishes. To express our wants.

Communication has two parts, though, and one of them often gets overlooked: listening. In some marriages, one partner talks easily and unceasingly but never stops to let the other person talk. One talks and the other listens, and that's almost as bad as nobody sharing.

Sometimes I suggest a kitchen timer for couples with this problem and recommend that they use it for a while just to become aware of their patterns. One talks for five minutes, and when the timer dings, the other talks.

One wife complained that her husband talked too slowly, with such great long pauses between words that he said practically nothing before his five minutes were up. We joked about requiring the timing to be done like football or basketball, where the clock moves only when there is action going on. Talking for five minutes might take that man fifteen minutes! He suggested taking seven minutes to her five, because it took him longer to think about what he wanted to say.

Anything can be accomplished when both people are looking to cooperate. *Nothing* can be accomplished when one or both are not cooperating.

When Talking Isn't Working

What if you're a couple who already talks a lot but still has long unresolved problems? You have to do what marriage counselors do: Find the short circuit in the connection.

When we seem unable to arrive at new workable solutions, we need to see clearly what approaches we've tried so we can shift gears and try a different approach. Most of us tend to find a favorite tactic and stick with it come hell or high water. (Never mind that it hasn't helped yet; it should work!)

"I've told him and told him to pick up his dirty laundry, but do you think he ever does it on his own? No! I have to keep telling him!"

That kind of technique is more common than you would believe. We tell and tell, remind a thousand times, and tell some more, all the while complaining that we shouldn't have to remind.

> No one is going to change his or her behavior just because someone *says* to change it.

We *don't* have to remind. Of course we can continue that process for the rest of our married lives if it suits us. But we need to be forewarned that the bad behavior will continue just as long. No one is going to change his or her behavior just because someone *says* to change it.

So what happens if a wife decides not to keep on with the first option of reminding her husband to pick up his clothes?

Option number two could be deciding that it isn't worth the hassle. She'll just pick up the dirty laundry herself and save her breath. But she'll probably be mad as a hornet and punish him in some other way.

Option number three might be an honest explanation of how his habit makes her feel, and a request for help in solving it. "Sweetie, when you leave your dirty laundry on the floor, I feel really annoyed (or miffed, exasperated, disappointed, resentful, angry, or whatever fits best) because I don't want to pick it up, nor do I want to keep reminding you. When can we talk about this issue?"

Respectful Confrontation

One of my favorite tried-and-true formulas for opening discussions that need to be had is the following: "When you . . . I feel . . . because . . ." It's not *guaranteed* to be effective, and I can't promise that the other party won't get angry, but it's the most respectful confrontation I know of, and you must start somewhere. Here are some more examples:

"*When you* get upset at my every request, *I feel* sorry for myself *because* it gets in the way of finding solutions or compromises."

"*When you* scold the kids at the dinner table, *I feel* sorry for them and mad at you *because* dinner should be a pleasant time for us."

"*When you* forget my birthday, *I feel* devastated *because* it's the one day of the year I want to be treated specially."

"*When you* make jokes about my weight in front of guests, *I feel* furious *because* it's cruel to embarrass someone."

Recently, I added a fourth step to the communication formula I'm so fond of: "Would you be willing to . . . ?" For example:

"*When you* accept a dinner invitation for us without asking me, *I feel* angry *because* I want to make my own decision. *Would you be willing to* check with me before committing for me?"

More examples:

"*When you* read the mail while I'm telling you something, *I feel* hurt *because* I feel shut out and unimportant. *Would you be willing to* wait until I finish my story?"

"*When you* leave the cupboard doors open, *I feel* annoyed *because* it looks so cluttered and I might bump my head. *Would you be willing to* close them when you get something out?"

Salespeople are taught always to ask for the sale. When they've described the item and the price, they need to specifically ask something like "May I wrap one of these up for you?"

Just telling someone our thoughts and feelings might not be enough to get the point across. Asking if they're willing to act differently shows we want an answer. Granted, the answer might be "No." So then we have to continue the discussion or drop it for a while—but we can always come back to it later.

Testing the Water for Talk

Just because one person is ready to talk doesn't necessarily mean the other is. And if the temperature isn't right, good sense tells us to back off—but only temporarily. Too often we back off altogether and never resume the conversation that really needs to be had.

For example, someone might say, "Hey, I told her I don't like the way she corrects me when I'm telling something to our friends, but she got mad right away and that was the end of that."

We tend to let things "end" prematurely when they're not really ended. We're still carrying around unresolved anger and hostility.

We positively must communicate as long as it takes to reach some resolution, but it doesn't have to be all at once! There is no time limit. We can solve a difference of opinion in one minute or one month or twenty years, but the important thing is to continue working on it. We get defeated too easily. Persistence is essential, but so is consideration for the other's feelings—honesty with kindness.

If the man is in bed with the flu and a raging fever, that's not a good time for the woman to say, "When you interrupt me, I feel annoyed because you seem to think what I'm saying is not important."

> We can solve a difference of opinion in one minute or one month or twenty years, but the important thing is to continue working on it.

She's a hundred percent right in making that statement, but it can't get far in the face of the flu. Hopefully she'll broach it when he's feeling better.

Even then, we can be pretty sure he won't say, "Why, darling girl, thanks for telling me. I was a beast to do that. It'll never happen again." Life just isn't that easy! He might, however, be receptive to communicating and say, "I didn't know I ever interrupted you. When did I do that?"

She might be tempted to answer, "You always do that," because she may have been keenly aware of it many times. But few things happen "always," and exaggerating won't help solve the problem.

A specific incident would help. "Last night when your sister was here and I was telling her how I make raspberry vinaigrette, you just started showing her that new book you bought."

He might apologize, which would be lovely, and the whole issue can be dropped. But let's say he doesn't. He might excuse his behavior with, "I thought you were through."

"I wasn't."

Now is a good time for her to "ask for the sale," to define what she wants from him. "At any rate, could we agree that neither of us will interrupt the other one?"

"Sure."

"Great. Thanks."

That's how communication could happen. Wouldn't it be grand to get things taken care of so quickly? But you and I both know that too often things don't go that smoothly.

What if he had bristled and attacked with, "I suppose you think you never interrupt me?" or "Well, maybe if you wouldn't talk nonstop all the time I wouldn't have to interrupt," or "Nobody cares about your vinegar anyway," or "Oh, boy, here we go again. I never do anything right, do I?" or "What is this, lecture number ninety-four?" or something like that. There are millions of snappy retorts along those lines, and we've all heard them many times.

That response is a cue that the pool water is not the right temperature. He is not going to be a cooperative communicator, or so it appears. She might try again.

"Look, I'm trying to be respectful and tell you my feelings about something that's important to me. Would you be respectful, too, and not get sarcastic?"

If she says that in a calm voice, there is a chance he'll back off and be more open to cooperation. If so, great—go ahead. If not, define feelings again.

"When you refuse to discuss problems, I feel really discouraged because we'll never get our differences settled unless we talk about them. But I'm certainly willing to wait until later to talk about it. When can we talk about it?"

"Why do we have to talk about problems all the time? You make life so unpleasant."

"I just want to settle this one problem if we can. How about after dinner? Tonight? Tomorrow? You decide."

That's a respectful way to approach a person who wants to avoid discussing unpleasant subjects (which includes a large part of the population, by the way). Sometimes it elicits an, "Oh, well, let's talk about it now." But sometimes not. The point is, we have to be persistent if we're dealing with someone who prefers to avoid uncomfortable issues.

We need to keep reminding ourselves that it is truly impossible for us to change our mates—we can change only ourselves.

It's doing no favor to anyone to sigh, martyrlike, and say with resignation, "Oh, never mind. It wouldn't do any good anyway." We can't let ourselves have the luxury of "letting it go" and feeling superior. That just enables us to chalk up another unresolved hurt and heap another coal on the fire of resentment. We *have* to keep trying if we're to have any hope of improving our relationship.

By the time people are old enough to marry, they've established patterns that are so deeply imbedded it can be awfully hard to change them. Indeed they can *seem* impossible to change. We need to keep reminding ourselves that it is truly impossible for us to change our mates—we can change only ourselves. But they certainly have the capacity to change themselves, if they choose to.

If they choose to. That's a biggie.

Choice

If my behavior is working for me, getting all my needs met and avoiding unpleasant issues, then I'm probably not going to want to change. Change comes only when my discomfort is sufficient to warrant it.

That's why the wife who complains "I've told him and told him and told him to pick up his dirty laundry" is still having to pick it up herself. Her husband, that smart man, discovered long ago that he can survive the barrage of reminders very well. And, it's a small price to pay for getting out of picking up his dirty clothes. Why should he change? To him the end result would be negative, not positive. He likes it better this way.

For him even to *want* to change, there would have to be a good reason. How can his wife find a reason?

Honesty, communication, and persistence. Being perfectly honest and nonmanipulative, she would express her feelings. "Honey, I'm tired of being a nag. I am quitting as of this minute telling you to pick up your dirty laundry. That has to be your decision. In fact, I apologize for nagging you about it all these months (or years). But I won't pick it up, either, because if I did, I'd get resentful and punish you in some other way. I'll wash anything that's in the hamper. So, if your clothes aren't there, they'll just stay dirty, *OK?*"

My guess is the husband would be so delighted to hear this, he'd grin broadly and say, "Great, doll!" and maybe even give her a smooch.

She could feel a marvelous sense of freedom from this annoying nuisance to which she'd chained herself all that time. She returns his affection with enthusiasm, knowing she's no longer responsible for his laundry.

Let's imagine the scenario. As the days go by, their bedroom becomes strewn with dirty shirts, pants, socks, underwear, running shorts, swimming trunks, and sweaty headbands. She's keenly aware of the rising heaps of mounting laundry, but she's unaffected. She just watches the process occur.

One or two hitches might happen, such as when he says, "Babe, I need a white shirt for the banquet tonight, and they're all dirty. Can you wash one for me?"

Her immediate response might be, "No white shirts? Whose fault is that? You'd have white shirts if you'd just dropped them in the hamper. But no, you can't be bothered with details like that.

See what happens when I turn over some responsibility to you? Ha! Now you know why I told you and told you to pick up your laundry. You are so helpless! I can't believe you've let all these clothes pile up. What a slob!"

But if she indulges in that tirade, it means she hasn't changed herself. She's just put her feelings on temporary hold. If she has changed, she would see it very differently. She is no longer responsible. It's his problem. He's quite able to figure out for himself a few options that will get him through, but that's his job, not hers.

If I were she I'd say something like, "Oh, that's too bad they're all dirty. No, I'm not washing clothes today; I have a lot of other things to do." And I'd leave the room. No need standing there to hash it all over. No need to make suggestions, such as "Maybe you could wash your own shirt or even buy a new white shirt today." He can think of that all by himself. Or he can dig through the pile and pull out a dirty white shirt to wear to the banquet. That's his right.

If she thinks, "I can't stand being with him at the banquet if he's wearing a dirty shirt," she has the right to stay home. However, chances are she could stand it very well.

He might get angry with her for not having the shirt clean, but he has full rights to any feelings he chooses to indulge in, and she can stand that, too.

> **When we're part of the solution, we're way more willing to cooperate than when someone makes decisions for us.**

Now, the process of change has just begun, and there are still myriad details to work out. I know wives reading this are thinking, "Yeah, my husband would stack up dirty clothes until he ran out of things to wear, then dump them all in the wash at once. It would take me two solid days of doing laundry to catch up. No thanks!"

One of the options there is this: "Love, I need to tell you my feelings about your dirty clothes. I'm not willing to have a giant stack of them dumped in the hamper all at once for me to spend two days working on. I know you don't like picking them up as you go along, and I don't like being responsible for them. We need to find other ways to handle this. Do you have any suggestions?"

Asking our mates for their input is often amazingly effective. When we're part of the solution, we're way more willing to cooperate than when someone makes decisions for us.

Another option is this: "I don't want to wash more than two loads a week (or whatever is appropriate). How about doing your own laundry? Then you can let it pile up as long as you want."

That means letting him handle it any way he wants. One wife reported that her husband opted to take it all to a laundry once a month and the bill was enormous. We have to be willing to let that happen. We can't have control of our spouse's behavior. There will always be things we disapprove of, and money spent is a big issue. But still there has been a change in behavior, which is what we're looking for.

This is not manipulation because it's up-front and honest.

It's not game playing. It's simply defining what you will and will not do.

"You Decide"

There are many other variations on this course of action, and you might want to talk about them together. It's not a technique that's meant to cause more resentment. Conversing about it is permissible and even advisable, so long as it's not the old routine of "telling him and telling him."

It might include "Sweetie, this bedroom is getting a dreadful stench about it from your sweaty laundry. I'm having trouble sleeping in here. Maybe you could move your stuff out to the back porch or garage or basement, or I could sleep in the guest room . . . you decide."

I love the phrase "you decide." It gives a lot of freedom to the other person, and it's respectful. I can tell you my decisions in the matter and you can decide what you prefer.

One very big caution: Don't let this method become a power struggle. Marriages can end over both parties becoming so determined to win that solution-finding takes a back seat to battle strategies.

Remember: *Nobody wins in a power struggle.* The focus should be strictly on finding an acceptable resolution, not on punishing the guilty party.

Short Circuits

Getting into a power struggle is just one way of short-circuiting the communication process. We need to keep an eye out for any short circuit that prevents resolution. The most frequent offenders are these:

1. Judging the other person as "bad" or "wrong," and therefore deserving of punishment.

Instead, take the approach that you have a common problem or difference between you that needs to be solved.

2. Going for a victory, being determined to "win."

Instead, focus on cooperating, not competing. You stand a much better chance of working through every difficulty when you work together. Power struggles only divide you further.

3. Manipulating, trying to change the other's attitudes and behavior by using your emotions to affect their feelings.

Instead, you need to talk *and* listen, for as long as it takes (though it doesn't have to be nonstop) with honest disclosures of feelings and hopes, defining what you'd like.

continues

4. Withdrawing, distancing, refusing to get involved at all. This may be the most powerful position of all. It's impossible for the spouse of a close-mouthed, totally noncommunicative person to achieve any kind of resolution. Although we may judge the silent person as "weak," we must recognize the relentless strength demonstrated by refusing to talk, which leaves the other partner virtually helpless.

Instead, you need to be willing to communicate respectfully, in order to maintain *any* relationship!

There are, no doubt, many variations on all these faulty circuits, and probably many other flaws I haven't defined. But these are the ones I come across most often in my practice.

Expressing Emotion versus Solving a Problem

Fighting is one of the biggest wastes of time and energy. When there is fighting, there is a power struggle. And nobody wins in a power struggle.

I know a lot of people will disagree with me that fighting is wasteful. They usually protest, "But it's unhealthy to keep anger inside. When you're upset, you have to let it all out." Sometimes they even add, "Otherwise you might get cancer."

I agree that bottling up anger is unhealthy. So how do we release anger without fighting? It can be done very effectively, and it doesn't need an audience. In fact, you can yell and scream and holler all alone and enjoy feeling free and uninhibited by spectators.

There are many things we do best when we're alone; going to the bathroom, for one thing. It's important for good health, but it's accomplished best without observers.

Releasing anger falls in the same category. If you think it's good for you, by all means, enjoy the process. But don't expect anyone to stay in the room with you.

I maintain that nothing can be settled or resolved in the heat of emotion. There are two different areas of need (and I use the word "need" loosely) that we often mistakenly pursue at the same time; the need to express emotion and the need to solve a problem. It may sound like an efficient use of time to work on both needs concurrently, but it just isn't effective. The problem-solving gets shoved aside in the face of the emotion-releasing.

I tell my clients this: As soon as one of you raises your voice in anger or starts to cry, then shelve the issue you're working on. Leave the room and allow your feelings to surface. Cry as long and hard as you feel like crying. Kick a tree, run furiously around the block six times, beat on a mattress, or shout cuss words in your basement—give in thoroughly to venting emotion until you're spent.

> I maintain that nothing can be settled or resolved in the heat of emotion.

Then blow your nose, bandage your foot (where you kicked the tree), have a nice drink of water, and come back to the conversation. With clear minds and healthy bodies, you can again look for solutions. But the minute either person feels tears or anger welling up, repeat the process.

"You have to be kidding," clients say. "That would take forever."

So? There is no rush. Trying to find understanding or compassion or answers would also take forever in the face of anger or tears—and any solutions you did find would probably be less than satisfactory.

You wouldn't try to wash your car and make an omelet at the same time. Both are worthy activities, but they can't be done simultaneously. Once we recognize that it's logical to separate anger-releasing from problem-solving, we can incorporate that same thinking in our communication.

> My views on fighting are based on the feelings I have when someone verbally attacks me and anger surges up as a result. In that state, I've never felt a desire to cooperate and lovingly search for compromise and understanding.

It might be difficult at first, but that's OK. Again, there is no rush. When either of you can remember to try the new process, you'll gradually find it gets easier.

The danger, now, is that the one who remembers you can't do both things at once might want to lord it over the other one. "Nyaa, nyaa, nyaa, Lee Schnebly says we can't talk if one person is crying or shouting, so I'm going to the movies, nyaa, nyaa." It could become just one more form of manipulation or power or withdrawal. Isn't it amazing how many ways we can find to mess up a relationship?

I know my beliefs will be vehemently rejected by many people who believe down to their toes that fighting is good. They feel cleansed by a good heated exchange, and it has, in fact, enhanced their marriages. I never argue with success. If you're one of those people who enjoys a good scrap and you're married to another, you have my sincere blessings and admiration for taking a behavior that could be destructive and making it a positive force in your lives. Don't even *consider* changing if you're both enjoying your relationship the way it is.

The suggestions I make are for people whose lives together aren't working the way they want them to. My views on fighting are based on the feelings I have when someone verbally attacks me and anger surges up as a result. In that state, I've never felt a desire to cooperate and lovingly search for compromise and understanding. I doubt that many people feel much differently. Anger begets anger.

But that's not to say that I believe in being a wimp and pussyfooting around an uncomfortable situation. Acting like everything is fine when you're a churning mass of hurt or anger inside would be even more damaging than a temper tantrum.

I guess the element I think of as being most important is *respect*. I want to tell you what's wrong in my life. I want you to know what you did that disappointed me. You deserve to hear what I would like in place of that behavior. You need to know what makes me sad, mad, glad or scared if we're to have a good working relationship. But I want to tell you all those things in a respectful way, not an attacking way. Attacks hurt, and I don't want to hurt anyone—especially the people I live with.

It's perfectly appropriate to say, "I am so angry right now that I don't want to try to talk about it. I'd say hurtful things. Let me cool down a while, then I'll be able to talk rationally."

The same is true if I'm crying. It's fine to say, "Boo hoo, sob sob . . . Let me cry for a while and *then* we can talk, sniff, sniff."

A marvelous way of discovering what causes the short circuits in your own patterns of communication is to tape-record your conversations. Larry and I tried that once, and it got so funny we finally laughed and stopped the recorder. Both of us were being so careful to talk "right" that we weren't being ourselves at all. We were caught up in jargon like, "Do I hear you saying that . . ." and "I can't argue with your feelings, but my belief is. . . . "

Playing it back, we roared at the phoniness of the dialogue, but we certainly had been in good control of ourselves.

You probably don't need a tape recorder. You already know who gets mad and yells, who cries, who withdraws, who uses sarcasm, and so on. All you need to do now is decide to switch that behavior for a new kind.

Sometimes it's fun to switch roles. You both do what the other one normally does. The crier now yells and screams. The yeller cries or doesn't respond—all in the name of scientific experimentation. Of course nothing gets straightened out that way, but it does shed light on the other person's feelings. That's worth something.

A Lifelong Process

We need to keep in mind, however, that *getting* our needs met is a lifelong process. Few of us ever get to say, "There now. My needs in this relationship are all met, and there they'll stay."

It would be easier if we didn't change so much, but we do. What I wanted in a mate at twenty is a far cry from what I want now. And I suspect my ideals will continue changing to my grave.

The positive thought, though, is that the skills we develop in getting our needs met will be useful every day. Like riding a bike, we'll never forget how. Unlike riding a bike, we're called upon to use these skills constantly, so they should keep sharpening themselves. I haven't been on a bike in years, but I converse daily.

Sometimes people ask Larry, "Doesn't it drive you crazy to be married to a counselor? She must know all the tricks."

Sometimes Larry has agreed with fervent desperation. Many times both of us have wondered if our marriage was the right one. Would life have been easier if we'd married someone else?

Both of us (fortunately) agree that it probably wouldn't have. We'd have different spouses with different problems to deal with, but we'd still have problems. Marriage is just hard, that's all. But not impossibly hard. Maybe we should be glad it's so challenging, because it demands that we keep growing.

Sometimes I compare it to two rough stones put into a rock polisher. The very abrasiveness of the process makes the rocks smooth and shiny, and much more beautiful than they were before.

There are no "tricks" to a happy marriage, but there are some skills that can help make the process much less frustrating and more productive. All of them have the same base: Being willing to communicate with honesty and respect. That's it in a nutshell.

Talk It Over

1. Each person make a list of things your partner does that irritate you, frighten you, or make you feel hurt, suspicious, or resentful.

For example:

> **I don't like it when you . . .**
>> · drive too fast
>>
>> · criticize me in front of the children
>>
>> · make fun of me in front of friends
>>
>> · don't pay attention to what I'm saying

2. Now write down the desire that goes with each complaint. For example:

> **I would like to . . .**
>> · feel safe and relaxed when you're driving
>>
>> · always feel the children respect me
>>
>> · not feel embarrassed in front of others
>>
>> · know that what I have to say is important to you, that I am important to you

3. Next write the *specific* request that would help satisfy each desire.

For example:

> **Request:**
>> · When you're driving, I'd like you to obey the speed limit.
>>
>> · Please tell me your complaints about me in private.
>>
>> · Look at me and listen when I speak. Let me know if you can't listen for some reason and why.

4. Identify what your partner is *already doing* that pleases you by finishing the following sentence with as many things as you can think of:

> **I feel loved and cared about when you . . .**

Examples:
- let me read the first section of the newspaper first
- tell me things you experienced during the day
- give me a back rub
- ask if I need something from the store
- check with me first before making plans
- compliment the way I look
- look at me when we talk

5. On another sheet complete this sentence:

I used to feel loved and cared about when you . . .

Examples:
- called me a pet name
- held my hand as we walked
- called me during the day to say you loved me
- wrote me love notes
- cooked my favorite foods

6. Think of some caring behaviors that you've wanted but never asked for.

I would like you to . . .

Examples:
- take a shower with me
- go for walks with me at least once a week
- initiate our love-making a couple times a month

7. Exchange lists, examine your partner's, and put a checkmark by any you're not willing to do at this time. Starting tomorrow, do at least two of the remaining ones each day for two months, starting with those that are easiest for you to do. Add more items as they occur to you. When your partner does a caring act for you, be sure to acknowledge it.

8

I Long to Be Close to You

Cinderella never had sex. She got all dressed up, went to the ball, and charmed the socks off the handsome prince, who whisked her off to the castle. Then for the rest of their lives, he worshipped her, agreed with her, hugged her often, kissed her tenderly, held her close as they talked hour after hour, chuckled warmly at her cute ways, and made her happy. She was the princess. He was the prince put into this world to make her happy ever after!

Though that concept may be a bit ridiculous, many women unconsciously expect marriage to be that way. Many of us were totally unaware of the expectations our husbands had been entertaining. While we were fantasizing about being Cinderella in the castle, the boys were busy with their own fantasies. In theirs, Cinderella was a real sexpot. She couldn't wait to hop off the horse, race the prince to the castle garret, and begin an outrageous striptease to the tune of *The Stripper*. That was only the beginning of the passionate sex life they would enjoy forevermore, in which she couldn't keep her hands off his body. She would be his own Playboy bunny—aggressive, seductive, and sultry. She would combine these traits with others that would be helpful to his career. She would also be a gourmet cook, a kind of combination Julia Roberts and Julia Child.

Common Sexual Problems

Because today's young wives see love, sex, and marriage far differently from the way their mothers viewed them, we might think young women sail into marriage with nary a misconception. But alas, it doesn't work that way. Cinderella and the prince live on in a neverending clash of *shoulds* that both partners still bring to the wedding.

Forbidden Fruit

Our expectations are part of the problem. One is the old appeal of forbidden fruit. All of us want what we can't have. Conversely we often *don't* want what we should have. Recently, a bride of less than a year poured out her hurt and confusion in my office. "Tom and I couldn't get enough sex before we were married. We slept together the first night we met and several times a day after that. We lived in his apartment for four months before the wedding. Our sex life was unbelievable. But right after we got married, he cooled almost immediately. Now he hardly touches me!"

Tom said, "If Margie would just quit hounding me for sex, I probably would want her again. But by now it's such a big 'should' that it's no fun. The more she nags me, the more I turn off."

Tom and Margie came from religious homes. Both felt guilty, even while they enjoyed their fantastic premarital sex. Once it was approved, it lost much of its appeal for Tom. Some people love a challenge. When the challenge goes, so does the lust. Furthermore, it became a power struggle to each of them. Each tried to make the other behave in the way they "should."

I Saved Myself for This?

Couples who remain virgins until the marriage bed sometimes feel disappointed after "saving" themselves all that time while they read about the fireworks that await them. Sometimes the actual experience doesn't measure up to the almost unbearable ecstasy they imagined. They feel cheated, discouraged, and angry with each other.

"It just isn't as exciting as I thought it would be," they say.

Intimacy and Desire

The very intimacy of marriage can also detract from sexual desire. The dashing young man who visits Pam in her apartment is pure excitement with his flowers, gifts, and bottles of good wine. The scent of his shave lotion thrills her, as does his sparkling conversation and even the tone of his voice. His touch is magic and his gaze electric. Simply being in his presence is an automatic turn-on. The thrill of his kisses makes him totally irresistible. The physical attraction is constant and insatiable.

Then comes the wedding and the total togetherness and the beginning of disillusionment. Pam begins to resent little habits she wasn't aware of before. She misses the flowers, gifts, and bottles of wine. There are few surprises anymore. There's criticism, arguing, and disapproval. His touch is no longer an automatic turn-on, but a demand. She bristles at it sometimes.

Though the pilot light is not necessarily out, it is definitely flickering.

Our grandmothers used to say, "Familiarity breeds contempt." Only determined couples can keep sex fun and exciting in spite of constant familiarity. Most of us thought it would be fun and exciting forever, or we wouldn't have agreed to marry in the first place. Is there a solution? I don't think so.

Maybe disillusionment is part of a giant Master Plan to keep civilization going. Maybe we need our naive attitude of hope and expectation or no one would ever marry. But whether or not we need it, I'm convinced we'll always have it. Hope springs eternal.

Our expectations cause us some disappointment. So what? Sex is no

All of us want what we can't have. Conversely we often *don't* want what we should have.

different from anything else. As we live and grow, we discover many expectations can cause us disappointment. It's one of those lessons we learn only by experiencing it frequently enough.

Differing Sexual Needs

Another problem in sexuality is the variety of different needs we have. So many disenchanted young wives tell me, "All he thinks of is sex! I want to be held and kissed and hugged. But for him, it always leads to the bedroom. I want love, but he just wants sex."

The husbands look confused and say, "Isn't that what marriage is for? Of course I want sex. Adults who love each other should want sex. I love my wife. I just can't understand her not wanting sex as much as I do."

I think they're both right. There's a lot of truth to the statement, "Men use love to get sex and women use sex to get love." Of course women enjoy good sex and men genuinely love their wives. But I think the thrust of their focus is biologically different.

Often a wife will express a wish to simply be held "with no strings attached." She doesn't want sex—only a gentle tenderness that will make her feel close and loved.

> Only determined couples can keep sex fun and exciting in spite of constant familiarity.

And the husband will shrug and say, "Well, sure, if that's all she wants, I can do that. I'll be glad just to hold her with no strings attached." And he means it sincerely. He loves his wife, and if it will make her happy, he's glad to oblige.

Later that evening he joins her on the sofa just to hold her. She's delighted! She snuggles warmly and thinks, "This is what life is all about. Oh, this is lovely! I feel so warm, secure, content and loved!" And just about then she feels his hand on her breast, hears his breathing get heavy, and sees hunger in his eyes. A stab of resentment goes through her. He promised! He said no strings attached, and now he wants to go to bed. No fair! She pulls away in disappointment, sees the rejection and hurt in his face, and she feels guilty.

Sometimes she goes ahead with it and they have sex. But she feels cheated of the pure, undemanding tenderness she had expected him to provide. Or she may refuse sex and he feels rejected, unloved, hurt, and angry. Either or both end up unhappy.

What happens then? They may begin to avoid these situations to avoid the potential hurt. The wife may find any number of chores to do in the evening so she won't appear idle and inviting. The husband may hesitate to make any overtures at all rather than risk rejection.

We believe if we really love each other, we should both want to make love at the same instant, with the same regularity.

Both feel like failures. They're just two normal people with feelings like everyone else. The problem is that one has a quicker turn-on point than the other.

It can work both ways. I've encountered more women who complain of overly ardent husbands, but many women complain their husbands won't turn on no matter how flimsy their nightgowns or how many hints they toss out.

I'm convinced one partner or the other always has a higher sex drive. So what's the big deal? Why is it any worse if one has a bigger appetite than the other?

It's all right for a couple to go to dinner and order what they want. For him, a giant slab of prime rib complete with baked potato, sour cream, fried zucchini, salad with roquefort dressing, garlic bread, and apple pie with ice cream. For her, a Chinese chicken salad. We never question the difference in food appetites, but somehow we feel there's something wrong if our sexual appetites differ.

We believe if we really love each other, we should both want to make love at the same instant, with the same regularity. And if we don't, we feel angry, guilty, hurt—or all three.

It seems to me the obvious solution is to think of sex the way we think of food. If Larry loves rice pudding every night and I don't, nothing prevents me from fixing it for him. I'll be glad to give him rice pudding frequently, if he wants it, as long as he doesn't insist I have some, too. From time to time I might decide rice pudding looks pretty good and I'll have a dish myself. But you can be sure if he *demands* rice pudding or lays a guilt trip on me because I don't want any, I may starve to death before I'll eat any. I may even stop providing it for him.

Some good friends of ours have been married for thirty-five years. They've handled the "problem" of differing sexual appetites so well it never became a problem at all. They simply agreed years ago that their only obligation to each other was to "be there." Frequently, when one's desire is greater than the other's, both end up equally excited by just being there. If they don't, that's fine. One can be actively thrilled and the other simply pleased at cooperating. Feelings don't get hurt and egos don't get shattered because neither has any expectations or "shoulds."

Not infrequently my clients, almost always the women, complain they feel "used." Trudy said, "I stay home with the kids all day, and my only contact with the outside world might be other women at a community college class or a neighborhood meeting. Mike is at a huge office full of people all day long. Some of the women he talks to are gorgeous. I know he likes them. I feel like he gets turned on by them all day long, then comes home and expects me to satisfy all that desire. It's not love for me he's feeling, just pure physical lust for something feminine. I'm supposed to be available. Not only available, but willing and eager. Well, I'm sorry, but I'm not."

Mike denies the accusation, but his reassurances fall on deaf ears. It's possible Trudy is at least partly right because sometimes we do get excited by people other than our mates. We automatically turn to our mates without even questioning where the desire came from in the first place.

This won't be a problem if other things are going well. If there's an atmosphere of love, respect, and cooperation to begin with, the lovemaking feels natural and good to both parties. But if the communication and warmth are lacking, sex becomes questionable. Actually, sex *is* communication. When the communication is bad, sex is bad. When we improve our communication, we improve our sex lives.

The best solution to different sexual appetites is compromise. One couple who solved it beautifully were Janet and Vince.

Janet had a fairly low sex drive, while Vince seemed to think about nothing else. When I asked him how often they thought they'd like sex if it were up to them, Janet piped up, "Once a month," just as Vince was saying, "Three times a day!"

What they did was find a number in between the two extremes. It took a lot of communication and discussion. Their reasoning was so skilled it would have made any debate team sit up and take notice. But they finally settled on "every four days."

It was considerably more often than Janet would have liked. But the agreement included the fact she could lie there and think about anything she wanted during the process because Vince was the one who "needed" sex. Because they really loved each other and wanted to cooperate, the solution was fine.

Another couple had the same problem in reverse. Jennifer was the physically affectionate one. Bill was relatively disinterested. In their case, we added manual stimulation: a vibrator. Jennifer was the one who wanted orgasm frequently, so she was delighted to have him apply the vibrator. In no time at all she reached a climax. Granted, it wasn't the proverbial "web of ecstasy," but it was satisfying nonetheless. Bill agreed he would satisfy Jennifer twice a week by whatever means he chose. He used the vibrator when he didn't feel like getting more involved himself.

Some people object to compromise and negotiation in sex on the grounds it takes the joy and spontaneity out of romance. It makes sex a business agreement instead of an act of love. But the people who are willing to try it generally find it solves their problems. As I said before, once we get involved, we often find ourselves turning on after all.

Resentment

Another fly in the ointment of sexuality is unexpressed resentment. I know from experience if I get angry with Larry and try to ignore it, pretend it isn't there, and refuse to deal with it, I store up resentment until wild horses couldn't drag me into his arms. Until the issue is resolved, I will be a reluctant bed partner, if one at all. I'd be like my friend Betty who, when her husband makes unwelcome overtures, says, "Oh, you wanta play rent-a-corpse tonight?" Making love with a cold, grim wife is hardly rewarding, although lots of men prefer it to the alternative of no sex at all.

Another problem with unexpressed resentment is it increases the chance of an affair. The longer I withhold my feelings from Larry, the more appealing it becomes to share those feelings with someone else. I become vulnerable and so does he. A kind, sensitive ear from someone else is often an irresistible invitation to something more. Actually, I use the word "irresistible" very loosely because I believe we can resist anything we want to resist. If we really want it, we like to convince ourselves we "just couldn't help it!"

Some people deliberately seek affairs to get even with their mates, as Marsha did. "I resented him so long and so hard, I had an affair just to show him I wasn't going to put up with his lack of attention. I wanted to hurt him badly. I knew it would hurt him more than anything else."

She was right. It did. The relationship was irreparably damaged, which was more than Marsha had intended.

Unresolved resentment takes its toll in a lot of other unsavory ways, including lack of desire, even impotence. When I work with an impotent husband, I almost always find some hostility toward his wife that needs to be resolved before the physical problem can be solved.

One husband maintained he couldn't have an erection with his wife, but he often awoke with one. Being able to have an erection at *any* time means impotence is not a physical impairment. We had to look at his relationship with his wife. Once we improved their communication and the quality of time they spent together, his impotence disappeared.

Unresolved resentment almost always interferes with good sex. People who are "pleasers" need everyone's approval so much they don't express their irritations. They don't get angry. They get even. What better way to punish the offending spouse than by disinterest in sex?

The best solution to unresolved resentment is letting our feelings out. I *have* to tell Larry when I'm annoyed, disappointed, or furious with him, even though I risk an argument, withdrawal, or whatever made me reluctant to rock the boat in the first place. If I remind myself I can stand his disapproval, our relationship will benefit from my honest complaints. I find it helps me to talk things out and get it over with. The longer I put off talking to him honestly, the longer I have no desire for closeness, warmth, or sex.

Power

Although sex is one of the last things that should ever become a power arena, it frequently does. Carol complains, "Sex seems like a victory to him. It's like he's won and I've lost. Even when he does nice things, I can see he's really just trying a gimmick so I'll give in. And when I do give in, I feel horrible afterward. I lie there and cry. I wonder why it isn't beautiful and rewarding anymore. Instead I'm just a challenge to his manhood. He proves he's macho by making love to me."

Though Carol could be misinterpreting her husband's intentions, chances are she's partially correct. We feel other people's attempts at power, although sometimes we don't recognize it as such. We just know it makes us mad.

People who are "pleasers" need everyone's approval so much they don't express their irritations. They don't get angry. They get even. What better way to punish the offending spouse than by disinterest in sex?

"Oughta wantas" are big in the sexual battleground. "You oughta wanta make love. Wives oughta wanta have sex," he says. She counters with, "You oughta wanta talk to me. You oughta wanta be close to me."

When each tries to control the other, nobody wins. Everyone loses in a power struggle. If you "win," it's only a temporary victory until the other party bests you. Yet, tonight in millions of bedrooms

> Tonight in millions of bedrooms around the world, people will compete, try to control one another, and try to be more powerful by demanding or refusing sex.

around the world, people will compete, try to control one another, and try to be more powerful by demanding or refusing sex.

The solution is to ask yourself if you're involved with that game. Sex and power can't survive simultaneously. Even in harmless games, like Monopoly or Scrabble, players often are sore losers. If you shoot for power in the bedroom, you automatically lose before you start.

How do you end the power struggle? One partner must be willing to withdraw from it. Share this insight with your partner, opening the subject for discussion. If that's too threatening, try changing your attitude, motivation, and behavior.

Competition and cooperation cannot coexist. A rich sexual relationship demands cooperation. If you tend to be a competitive person, you may be competing in your marriage or love relationship. If you are, your sex life is probably disconcerting. Make the decision to start cooperating instead. Treat your partner with respect, improve your communication, and get out of the one-upmanship game.

Trust

Sue and Andy came for counseling because their sex life was not what they wanted. "Sue seems to have a plastic shield around her," Andy complained. "She's fine when we're out for the evening with other people. She seems warm and happy. She even has a good time with me—until we reach our bedroom. Then she gets quiet, seems preoccupied, and withdraws from me completely. She builds this wall around herself."

Sue nodded in agreement, with a very sad expression. She seemed to be taking the blame, but she couldn't help what she was doing and felt bad about it.

We talked at length about feelings and attitudes. She told of her biggest fear. "I'm scared to death of being abandoned or rejected. I'll never forget the day my father walked out on my mother and how we all cried. Mother never got over it because she and my father had always been close. It came like a bolt from the blue. We had all trusted my father and we shouldn't have. He left us."

Sue's childhood decision was never to get into that bind herself. She avoided the risk by never getting too close to anyone.

But for sex to be good, there has to be trust. True, we're vulnerable when we trust. And some people prefer not to take that risk.

In Sue's case, we had to do some counseling before she became willing to take the risk. Once the decision was reached, she was able to let down her defenses and open up to Andy for the first time since they'd married.

Sometimes the reason for distrust is more recent and clear. "I was married before and my first husband wasn't trustworthy. He was fooling around with other women right from the start. Our marriage was just a handy place to come between affairs."

It's a fact: There are no guarantees in this world. We're always vulnerable to deceit or a change of heart that could lead to rejection. If that happens, we can stand it. Yet a lot of people are reluctant to believe in anything that chancy. Ages ago someone said, "It's better to have loved and lost than never to have loved at all." But tell that to a recent divorcée and watch her expression of disdain.

> Without a willingness to risk, to open up and be vulnerable, you'll never allow yourself to feel close to someone. Your sex life will be mediocre at best.

It boils down to an individual decision, one we must all make for ourselves. Without a willingness to risk, to open up and be vulnerable, you'll never allow yourself to feel close to someone. Your sex life will be mediocre at best.

Personally, I highly recommend the risk. When you love someone, you are vulnerable. You'll be hurt from time to time, but it's worth it when you're able to enjoy a really intimate relationship.

Performance Anxiety

Probably the all-time king-size problem in the sexual arena is performance. We worry about how our partner is going to evaluate us and whether we'll measure up to his or her expectations. What a shame anything so basic as sex has taken on so many fears of inadequacy. But it has. We experience fear of performance more than any other area of sexual dysfunction.

Debbie says plaintively, "The more educated we become, the more performance is demanded of us! It used to be that men were happy if their wives would 'just submit.' No more! Now they get upset and uptight if we don't have orgasms every time. Multiple orgasms, yet!

"They analyze our orgasms. My husband keeps asking, 'Did you have a vaginal orgasm or just a clitoral orgasm?' I'm sick of having my lovemaking analyzed all the time. I wish I could get away with 'just submitting' like my mother did!"

She has a realistic complaint. A husband may feel threatened if he can't send his wife into "webs of ecstasy," as a gothic novel might say. He is so concerned with perfection in lovemaking he may put pressure on his wife. This needlessly complicates the whole matter.

On a recent popular talk show, guests explained their research indicating women might be able to ejaculate during intercourse. While the largely feminine audience was interested in the presentation, one well-received comment was that now men will have yet another goal to pursue—finding the "magic button" to push so women could ejaculate.

"They've taken the magic out of romantic love," sighed one woman. "It's become a scientific skill." Someone else suggested what we need is more candlelight and wine, and fewer charts to follow. There was a feeling that men and women already have far too many "shoulds" around intercourse.

Perfectionism

Perhaps the biggest culprit behind our performance fears is the monster of perfectionism. "If I can't do something perfectly, I'm not going to try it at all." That attitude is crippling enough in other areas to cheat us out of a lot of pleasure, from reluctance to try new sports or new skills like guitar-playing to sex. But sex never has to be perfect to be enjoyable.

I love my friend George's statement: "When sex is good, it's just great. When sex is bad, it's still great!" George's wife is a lucky lady, with no pressures of performance and no expectations of perfection from her husband. George himself is equally lucky, with the freedom simply to enjoy and cooperate without measuring.

Once we start to measure the quality of our performance, we lose much of the pure pleasure we could be relishing. When we spend so much mental energy evaluating, we forfeit spontaneity.

But the worst penalty of perfectionistic evaluation is the fact we can *never* measure up! True perfection is impossible. We're doomed to a life of disappointment.

We need to lower our standards and apply the adage, "Have the courage to be imperfect." Quit worrying about performance. If you have to ask "How was it?" you're missing the whole point. As George says, "The worst sex I ever had was terrific!"

I'm not opposed to education, but I do think we might be taking sex education for adults a bit too seriously. There are thousands of cookbooks packed with hundreds of mouth-watering recipes, but no one ever expected us to try them all. In fact, most people are content with basic meat, potatoes, vegetable, bread, and dessert and, these days, many are just as happy with a frozen lasagna. People rarely ask, "Aren't you willing to try the Pork-and-Apple Oriental on page 68 of that new cookbook you got for your birthday?" And if any partner did ask, the answer would likely be a resounding, "Hell, no!" that would end the discussion then and there.

Not so with sex. "Dan says he and his wife read *The Delights of Sex* at bedtime and try a different page every night. Shall we do that?" Or "Honey, you're so conservative. There are hundreds of different positions. Why do you always want the same one or two or three?"

A wife might say, "My friend Julie can't wait till bedtime because Steve is so creative in his lovemaking. He thinks of such exciting erotic things to do, she just can't get enough!" Or "I love reading those romantic novels because the sex scenes sound really fantastic. Why don't we make love that way?"

The resulting feelings are the same for both sexes—threat and inadequacy. "I must be a lousy lover. I'm dull, uncreative, stodgy. I'm a miserable failure and will avoid the whole thing." Another way of responding might be, "Damn it, if I'm not a good enough lover at home, I'll have an affair and prove I'm terrific." Regardless of which gender is complaining, the reaction is the same. "Maybe I can't measure up." So in self-defense, we attack each other.

"You know what you are? Frigid!"

"If you were a decent lover I'd be fine!" Then both partners feel threatened by their "poor performance," which in reality might be perfectly good.

We're the best-educated generation there ever was. A price we pay for it is the awareness that anything can be improved. So we begin to feel inadequate. But education isn't the only cause. Plain old inferiority can also cause feelings of inadequacy.

"I have such small breasts. I'm ashamed to have my lover see them."

"I haven't had the experience most men have. How am I going to satisfy her?"

"I'm afraid I'll never be able to reach a climax. I'll die of embarrassment."

"I'm not big like a lot of guys."

The more we stew about it, the more apprehensive we become. Sometimes we're almost immobilized by feelings of inadequacy.

Morality

Another strong deterrent to our sexual enjoyment is the issue of morality. Even though we're adults and allowed to do all the things we couldn't wait to do "when we grow up," we're often stuck with the beliefs we formed as children. Many of the thoughts that plague us now are the result of attitudes our parents instilled in us for our protection or our own good.

We still have little tape players in our minds. They play endless tapes of old "shoulds" and "shouldn'ts" that influence our behavior and feelings, even when we're not aware of it. Complicating the problem is the fact that every one of us has different tapes. Yet most of us think our own beliefs are the "right" ones.

Many women grow up learning zilch about sex. Their mothers blushed at the very mention of the word and could hardly explain the physical process, let alone the emotional dynamics. As little girls, they quickly learned their parts "down there" were not to be touched or looked at. My own mother tried hard not to overreact when she saw Betty and me "playing nurse" behind the oleanders. But her very manner and expression as she called us in for cookies indicated great discomfort and shame. When I copied my brother's phrase, "They caught me with my pants down," my mother called me aside and told me quietly it wasn't a nice thing for a girl to say.

We grew up filled with doubts about the appropriateness of our sexuality. Each of us had to struggle with making our own codes and beliefs just as much as older women, though perhaps in different ways.

One moral code everybody agrees on, though, is that sex between husband and wife is perfectly appropriate and desirable, and is to be enjoyed. It seems we shouldn't have problems in that area, yet we do.

"He'd like oral sex and I think it's wrong."

"I'm ashamed I have fantasies about other men while I'm having intercourse with my husband."

"I feel guilty about using birth control because of my religion, so I never really enjoy sex."

"Even though I know it's all right now that I'm married, I still somehow feel dirty doing it."

"Sex with girlfriends and prostitutes is one thing. But I feel like my wife is so good and pure, I can't get turned on to her."

"I'm so dependent on my husband, he feels like a father figure. It seems incestuous to make love with him."

How do we deal with these moral dilemmas? Communication. We need to talk to our mates and express our fears, doubts, and concerns. We can consult many other sources for education and reassurance—our priests, ministers, rabbis, marriage counselors. Even books on the subject help us make our decisions.

In the end, making decisions is up to us. We can draw on all kinds of sources, but we have to decide for ourselves what we believe is right and wrong.

Once we determine what we believe, we have to do it—or not do it, as the case may be. Changing our beliefs doesn't automatically change our feelings in a jiffy. It takes time to get used to new beliefs and feelings.

If I decide I want to turn over a new leaf and become wildly erotic, experimenting with all sorts of sexual play, I have to give myself permission first. Then I have to plunge in and try it, even if I feel embarrassed and uncomfortable. Only by doing it will my feelings begin to change. Soon I may find myself really enjoying all the new behavior, but I won't ever enjoy it unless I start.

New feelings and behavior have to come from our own decision that we *want* to change, and that we believe it's OK. If someone else is trying to get me to change when I truly believe such behavior is wrong, I'll probably never enjoy it. It just won't work.

What do we do in a case like that? If one person in the marriage thinks oral sex is terrific and the other thinks it's dreadful, all we can do is approach the problem like any other problem. Try compromise and negotiation along with communication. "I'm willing to try oral sex if you'll paint the porch." Or "Gee, honey, in spite of all the books that encourage it and even though Father Doyle says it's fine, I still can't bring myself to do it. I'm really sorry . . . I guess we'll never be perfectly matched in every way, will we? But remember, even the worst sex is terrific!"

Other Sexual Problems

There are other problems in our sexual endeavors that may seem relatively unimportant. But they can be disheartening nonetheless.

Schedule Conflicts

"I'm a night person; he's a morning person. He falls asleep even before I get my teeth brushed, so we never get to make love at night. Then in the morning, he's grabbing for my parts while I'm still sound asleep. I get upset with him."

Solution? Compromise. "We make love two nights a week and two mornings a week." Or "This week we do it at night. Next week we do it mornings." That's fair and respectful.

Boredom

"Sex is boring. Always exactly the same." Sonia and Tim made up fantasies to tell each other and acted out the ones that were feasible. Tina and Chuck tried a few X-rated movies. Molly and Michael bought books on variation and technique. Boring sex is easy to liven up when both parties are willing to experiment.

Fear of Pregnancy

Another common complaint is, "I'm so afraid of getting pregnant I can't relax." That's a very real problem and one I won't try to solve. All you can do is investigate the different kinds of birth control that are available and find which is best for you. Take solace in the fact you'll eventually be past menopause. You'll never have to worry again. There are some advantages to age!

Children

"I'm so aware of the kids. I hear every little sound. I can't relax and enjoy sex when one of them is crying or calling for me."

That's a tough one. Generally, mothers are more in tune with their children's sounds because they spend more time taking care of them. It's difficult to turn off a feeling of responsibility. It's harder to let ourselves get into a sexual experience when we hear a child crying.

Here we need to consider frequency. If children are in the habit of crying or yelling for you often at night, you need to change your response pattern. If a child is in genuine need, you'll probably have to shatter the loving mood and go tend to him. Hopefully you can get the loving feelings back afterward.

I encourage parents to start closing their bedroom doors when their children are very young. You'll still be able to hear them if they cry or call out in need. But they'll grow up with the knowledge that parents enjoy privacy. Most parents leave the door open so they'll be able to hear what's going on. This can cause problems when the kids get older.

Mary Lou said, "As soon as Jim and I close the door to our bedroom, the kids gather right outside in the hall. They ask for snacks and wonder what we're doing. We can't relax with that going on!"

Indeed, they can't. Children should learn at an early age that parents need to be alone. But if you can't bring yourself to close your door all night every night, close yourselves in for short periods on a regular basis. Leave orders you're not to be disturbed unless it's an emergency. You don't have to make love every time, but you get the kids used to your privacy together so it will be accepted and taken for granted.

It's also good modeling for them. They'll know they deserve privacy when they're grown up and married.

Sex Isn't Everything

Although sex is important, it is not the most important thing in marriage. Sometimes we get so focused on our sexual problems, we lose sight of all the good things we have going for us. If you can take the pressure off by using some of these suggestions, do it. But recognize that sex alone doesn't determine the quality of a relationship.

I know many couples who deeply love each other. The joy they find in being together is beautiful to see. They have common interests, mutual respect, and senses of humor that keep the marriage well nourished. They have varying degrees of sexual incompatibility, but they accept those the way people accept any other problems in life. They make the best of the good things they have going for them.

I've known other couples who had superb sex lives. They enjoyed sex all the way to divorce court because there wasn't much else in their relationship.

I don't know of any couple who has a perfect sex life. We all have problems in that area. So if you have sex problems, isn't it nice to know you're normal? Relax and join the club.

Sexual Attitudes

Following is a list of common sexual attitudes, feelings, and problems to get you and your spouse talking about sex. Go through the list with your partner and each check off those that apply. When you have both gone through the list, talk about your responses. Which ones surprise you? Which ones can you change? How? How can your partner help you? How can you help your partner? Do you see a common theme to your responses?

- · I am afraid I will be disappointed with sex.
- · I usually just want to get it over with quickly.
- · I am afraid of getting too close to you.
- · You want more than I am able or willing to give.
- · I am afraid you will be disappointed with me.
- · I am too embarrassed to tell you what I want sexually.
- · I don't know what really feels good to me.
- · I can't or won't respond when you pressure me to have sex when I don't want to.
- · I feel like you use me to satisfy your sexual needs.
- · I can't get in the mood if you don't respond to me.

continues

- I have trouble relaxing.
- I often feel guilty or depressed following sex.
- I often feel so resentful that I cannot feel sexual or loving toward you.
- I resent when you don't want to have sex and I do.
- I sometimes wonder why anyone would want to have sex with me.
- I tighten up when I remember a past sexual experience.
- I turn off when you aren't sensitive to my wants and needs.
- Sex is too routine and boring.
- We don't have sex often enough.
- Sex seems like something you need to win. I do not like feeling as if I am giving in or losing.
- I am turned off by some things that turn you on.
- Withholding sex from you gives me a sense of power; it feels good to have something you want.

Other:

_____

_____

_____

_____

_____

9

No Other Love

No other?

Exactly how much do we have to forsake? That's a question we practically never think of before the wedding, because we can't imagine ever wanting to spend time with anyone but our beloved spouses-to-be. But in most marriages, the question arises sooner or later, because we're human.

Human beings have the capacity to love more than one person. Our children are good examples. We're sometimes surprised at how much we love each child, each in a little different way. They all have qualities and traits that differ from the others, and we value them for their differences as well as their similarities.

Our dear friend Bill McCartin used to say, "Love is not like jam, of which there's only so much to put on toast. Love is endless. We can love many people in many ways."

Perhaps that's both a blessing and a curse. It's fantastic to enjoy loving people. Sometimes it's catastrophic as well. But the problem isn't love, it's what we do with the love.

Defining Fidelity

Ideally we'd determine our beliefs about fidelity and make sure we agree before we get to the altar. Probably most of us assume both parties will be faithful. Some couples do discuss the issue and are easily able to promise fidelity, because in that state of euphoria they can't imagine being attracted to anyone else.

In some marriages the problem never arises. Often couples who share a strong religious bond keep themselves on the straight and narrow with never a thought of going astray. That's also true of many people without the spiritual backbone, who have a lot of integrity and would never allow themselves to do anything that goes against their moral or ethical values.

> Some couples do discuss the issue and are easily able to promise fidelity, because in that state of euphoria they can't imagine being attracted to anyone else.

At the other end of the spectrum are couples whose relationships are fraught with extramarital affairs that bring a lot of pain to one or both people involved, as well as to the "other person."

There are all kinds of variations in between. I know many couples who are living happily together with agreements vastly different from Larry's and mine. If what they do works for them, I can only applaud them, whether or not it matches my value system.

The Open Marriage

Years ago we met a couple that both of us immediately liked. They were pillars of their church, always heading up various committees and activities, as well as being excellent parents. And they were fun to be with. As we got to know them better, we learned a surprising fact: Both of them had continual affairs. They had been married some twenty years by then and had agreed from the start that one lover apiece would never be enough; they both preferred a variety. With that agreement they got married and have managed to continue that lifestyle ever since. They're still together, still happy, and still having affairs outside the marriage.

Unusual? For sure. How can it work? They agree and they're honest. There is no deceit going on. She'll announce at dinner, "I'll be spending Tuesday afternoons with my new boyfriend, so I won't be cooking those days."

He will nod agreeably and be happy for her, because he is enjoying Wednesday evenings with his girlfriend.

When they told us about their arrangement, we were more than a little incredulous, and I felt like a child learning the facts of life. I kept saying, "You do? He does? She is?" and feeling very naive that such a situation could be happening.

They went on to explain that they'd had to experiment a bit to work things out properly. They'd begun by being so honest they even told each other who the other parties were, but this caused some discomfort when they found themselves at the same social gatherings. So they discussed it some more and decided to keep names out of it but continue telling each other when something was going on.

Now, please don't get the impression that I'm recommending this! My misgivings about the whole situation include the obvious dangers like AIDS, as well as the ethics and morals concerning the other partners, what happens to them and their spouses, and all kinds of potential pain that I see as inevitable. I still find it totally amazing that it's worked between these two people, but they want it to work and have made it happen.

The Closed Marriage

Completely opposite from these people would be the couple who agree on no contact whatsoever with anyone of the opposite sex. One man I know refuses to let his wife go to the obstetrician alone. He insists on being there for each examination during her pregnancies as well as the actual birth. She must let no man into their home unless he's there, not even his brothers. He has a lot more freedom than she, incidentally, but both of them find that arrangement acceptable.

They seem as happy as the couple with the multiple sex partners.

It's not our job to judge any of these people and their choices. We need to focus our energies on deciding what we believe is fair and comfortable for ourselves.

Deciding What "Faithful" Means to You

Most folks, I think, agree that a husband and wife should be faithful to each other, and I think more couples honor that agreement than dishonor it. Certainly there is a lot of cheating in the world, but by and large it's not condoned by either the cheaters or the cheatees.

"It just happened; we didn't intend for it to happen" is a defense I hear quite a lot. Most of the time it goes against people's moral values to have an affair. Still, there are many individuals who truly believe an affair is acceptable if it happens out of town.

I have heard men and women alike confess to exciting rendezvous while they're away on business trips. Many of them subscribe to the adage, "What you don't know won't hurt you."

My opinion? It will hurt you. I personally believe that we can't beat the system.

I remember fondly one particular client who was most unsatisfied with a marriage that was practically sexless. Her husband spent most of his free time playing golf, the rest of it masturbating with magazines. His wife, whom I'll call Nancy, was frustrated and discouraged. She came in for counseling even though her husband refused.

Nancy was a travel agent and earned an all-expense-paid trip to Bermuda. When she got home, she came in for her appointment and was high as a kite on excitement and adventure. It was fun to see her so glowing, but I was concerned when she told me about the Australian she'd picked up in a bar and slept with.

"Nancy, that scares me to death," I said. "You didn't even know him. What if he had herpes or something?" (This was in the days before AIDS.)

Nancy shrugged with unconcern and said, "No problem; I already have herpes."

So that's great. Now the Australian might have taken herpes home to his unsuspecting wife.

Most of us try at some time to beat the system in some area, be it speeding or cheating on our income tax. Sometimes we get away with it. At least we don't always get caught. But in a larger sense, going against the rules does some damage to our self-esteem and our trust in other people.

The most paranoid people in the world are the cheaters. They don't trust *anybody!* Their attitude of distrust builds walls around themselves, keeping any kind of deep emotional relationship at arm's length. They look askance at people who maintain their innocence because they *know* people lie and cheat.

> The most paranoid people in the world are the cheaters. They don't trust *anybody!*

Why Do We Cheat?

What is cheating? An "affair" may mean different things to different people. In the old movie *An Affair to Remember,* two people fall in love and decide to marry but are kept apart for years by a tragic accident. Eventually they reunite and all is understood. It was a wonderful love story set in the 1950s, and there was no indication of physical sex between them. In those days, a love affair was usually the process of falling in love or being in love. Most of the time it led to marriage, and that is when the sex happened.

But that was the olden days. Today most people assume an affair includes sexual intercourse, so for now we'll use that definition.

Most of us would not condone or tolerate a spouse's cheating, and yet it seems to be a frequently occurring behavior. Certainly it's often discussed in marriage counselors' offices.

It Just Happened!

There seems to be a fairly common process involved. Typically the parties involved did not plan to have the affair. If I combined stories of the last thirty people who discussed the subject with me, I would come up with the following recitation. (I'll write it as if it's a woman talking, but it could just as easily be a man. Certainly it takes one of each to make it happen!)

We never meant for this to happen. I've worked in the same office with Don for four years. We've always been friends, but there was never anything more between us. We know each other's husband and wife, and we like each other. That's probably what troubles me more than any-thing else right now, knowing I'm hurting two people I re-ally care about.

I'm miserable. I've lost fourteen pounds, I can't sleep, I can't eat, and I have a constant knot in my stomach. Some-times I just wish I could get in the car and drive out of town; maybe go to California and start a new life with a new name and everything, but I couldn't because I love my kids too much.

Can you love two men? I honestly do love my husband, and I love Don, too. But the love I feel for my husband is not nearly as exciting. I mean, I care about him and don't want to hurt him, but with Don it's thrilling to be in the same room. Sometimes I wonder if I ever did love my husband, or if we just got married because it was the thing to do. I don't remember ever feeling this way to-ward him.

But the kids would just die if we got a divorce. The other night one of them asked me if Daddy and I would ever get divorced and I almost threw up. Don doesn't want a divorce either, because of his children.

There is no way I can resolve this situation without feeling a tremendous amount of pain. Whatever way I go is unbearable. I can't give Don up, but neither can I leave my husband and hurt the kids so much. They adore their daddy.

I feel so much compassion for clients who tell me this because they are clearly suffering. It is truly a no-win situation, with inevitable pain. It is listening to this pain so many times that makes me say, "It isn't worth it. You can't beat the system."

Naturally, I never say that to the person who is admitting this problem. He or she already knows it. I only say it *before* the fact if I get a chance.

Affairs almost always cause more pain than pleasure. But there are a thousand rationalizations for having them. It all boils down to one belief: I am entitled to have what I want.

One of my favorite movies is *A Touch of Class*, in which George Segal and Glenda Jackson play the parts of two strangers who start out with the intention of "a little good sex" and end up terribly in love and finally devastated at having to end the affair because he's married to someone else. It's a brilliantly acted comedy, but the end always makes me cry. I recommend it to anyone considering an affair.

Affairs almost always cause more pain than pleasure. But there are a thousand rationalizations for having them. It all boils down to one belief: I am entitled to have what I want.

I am every bit as susceptible to that mistaken belief as anyone else. I often convince myself I deserve what I want. Fortunately or unfortunately, the price I would have to pay usually jogs my better judgment. But not always. If I had thought about it yesterday, I wouldn't have pigged out at the Sunday brunch birthday party. This morning I groaned at the scale, announced it was time for severe self-deprivation and discipline, and went out for a brisk walk to prove I meant business. Regretful as I felt, though, I hurt nobody but myself.

With affairs it's different. Somebody else almost always gets hurt.

A "Bad" Marriage

One of the most common excuses I hear is, "If my marriage were good in the first place, I wouldn't have been susceptible to falling in love with someone else."

Maybe so. But practically all of us have marriages so "bad" from time to time that we're vulnerable. Certainly it's tempting to run into the arms of the nearest attractive person, but that doesn't solve anything. It's like having your car battery die and leaving the car to go steal someone else's. We would never do that; we'd get the battery recharged to put our own car back in working condition.

But that's logical reasoning, and falling in love is totally illogical. The feelings are overwhelming, no matter whom we're falling in love with.

> Certainly it's tempting to run into the arms of the nearest attractive person, but that doesn't solve anything. It's like having your car battery die and leaving the car to go steal someone else's.

I use the word "overwhelming" with some caution, however, because I think it almost gives us permission to do what we feel like doing. To be overwhelmed is to be helpless in the face of temptation, or whatever feeling is taking over. In truth I don't think we are ever out of control unless we let ourselves be.

I wish I had a nickel for every time I've developed a crush on another man. I fall in love very easily! So do lots of other people. But we all have the capacity to choose our behavior based on what will be best for us in the long run.

Boredom

Another common excuse for affairs is simply boredom. Most of us like a certain level of excitement in our lives, and when it's missing we look to fill it up with something. Few things are as exciting as affairs.

But few things are as exciting as hang gliding, either, or parachute jumping, and most of us don't get involved in those activities.

Having an affair is an easy high. How can anything that feels so good and is so easy to come by be resisted? Admittedly, sometimes it takes all the willpower we can conjure up. It's not easy. Staying faithful may be one of the biggest challenges we face.

We're so capable of convincing ourselves that it's okay to do whatever we feel like doing, that it's tough to convince ourselves it's *not* all right. Recently I heard someone say, "The greatest pain is caused by trying to hold onto the greatest pleasure."

This seems to ring true with affairs. The thrilling sensations and the excitement of forbidden fruit are almost too good to pass up. Those feelings are the greatest pleasures. We'd be crazy not to want them! But they do seem to cause the greatest pain. To avoid the pain, we must forego the pleasure.

Nobody said we get to have everything we want in life. Still, we can enjoy wanting whatever it is. Feelings are never right or wrong; only our behavior is.

Every morning I dutifully walk a brisk thirty or forty minutes, and my favorite route takes me to a nearby shopping center. You know why? Because there's a cinnamon-roll shop there that makes cinnamon rolls good enough to die for! I can sniff the scent in the air when I get close to the building, and it gets more and more enticing the closer I get to the shop. Finally, I walk right in front of it. I get to look in the windows and watch them rolling the dough and putting pats of butter along the strips,

> "The greatest pain is caused by trying to hold onto the greatest pleasure."

sprinkling them with cinnamon and sugar, and popping the pans into the oven. People are always inside eating rolls with their coffee and I glance at them with envy, but I continue walking. I do not go in, even though my heart and soul are there. Why don't I treat myself to a cinnamon roll? Because it would be bad for me. They must have a thousand calories each, and it wouldn't be worth the pain I'd feel as I got fatter and fatter—which is what would happen if I didn't discipline myself to avoid them.

So, in the long run, I'm happier not eating rolls than I would be eating them. I've eaten enough in my life to know the feelings of guilt and regret that follow, and I don't need those.

For me it's more positive to walk on by than to succumb. It's the same with men. They're sweet and spicy, and tantalizing and inviting, too, and I enjoy them with almost as much enthusiasm and gusto as I do cinnamon rolls. (Well, not quite so much.) But they're not for me to enjoy at a physical level. I don't need the pain.

To Prove We're Still Attractive

Sometimes we lean toward affairs in order to see if we've "still got it." Maybe we want to test our power and make sure we're still attractive to the opposite sex. Goodness knows we can look like death sometimes when we get up on an ordinary morning. In fact, I once heard a sermon that recommended this strategy to anyone whose spouse indulged in an affair: "Take a picture of your husband or wife first thing in the morning and mail it to the lover."

Certainly that would be the end of my affair, if I were to have one. I know my husband loves me if only because he's seen me in my faded flannel nightgown a million times and still calls me "Cutie!"

He and I laugh sometimes when we're all dressed up to go someplace, and we look at each other and say, "This is the real us!" We laugh because it is definitely not the real us. What is? Old worn nightclothes, soft old jeans, comfortable sweatshirts, and sneakers.

Comfort is wonderful. And yet it's the very thing that makes us hunger for excitement.

Friendship with the Opposite Sex

For me, the answer is friendship with men. It's the best of both worlds. I can revel in the comfort I feel with Larry. I don't have to act scintillating or look gorgeous. I'm free to be the real me in all my faded old clothes, and so is he. What a lovely freedom that is, not to have to impress.

On the other hand, it's fun to impress sometimes, both Larry and other people. I delight in getting dressed up and being sparkling. I like to be a little flirtatious. I like to turn on and feel attractive. It's fun to laugh and learn new things about new people. People are there for us to enjoy! God forbid that I ever take cinnamon rolls so for granted that I don't drink in the sight and scent when I walk by. God forbid, too, that I ever turn off the part of myself that notices and appreciates men.

But God forbid that I ever have an affair. It would spoil so many things. For one thing, I couldn't feel the confidence I now have to enjoy men without feeling any apprehension.

> Knowing I'm firmly in charge of my behavior frees me to have lunch with men friends as comfortably as I do with women friends.

If I felt I couldn't trust myself with another man, it would put a damper on any friendship I might have with one. Knowing I'm firmly in charge of my behavior frees me to have lunch with men friends as comfortably as I do with women friends.

"But why do you need to have lunch with men?" asked a client who was objecting to his wife's desire to do the same thing. "It only puts you in a dangerous position that you might not be strong enough to get out of. Why risk? Don't let yourself be tempted."

He has a point. There would be no alcoholics if people never took a drink. I don't think for a minute that people should drink if they can't control themselves. By the same token, they shouldn't have friends of the opposite sex if they doubt their ability to resist more than friendship. Each of us must make those decisions for ourselves.

But to answer the man's question, "Why risk it?" I would say this: Men and women are different in so many ways. What a shame it is to rule out half the human race just because they're the wrong sex. We learn and grow from spending time with people, and the more people we see, the more pleasure we enjoy.

Many of us are content enjoying the awareness of another person's general sexuality, without having to get involved with genital sexuality. The latter is what gets us in trouble.

Why do I like men? They have interesting appearances. I like looking at them. They often have good senses of humor, and I love to laugh. They have different perspectives on a lot of subjects and can be fun to argue with.

Why does Larry enjoy women? I asked him. "They have different viewpoints," he said after a moment's thought. "And having lunch with another woman gives me a chance to feel admired. Other women are not as honest with me as you are, so there's usually no criticism or negativity over lunch. That's nice."

I admit I blanched for a second at his answer. What, me? Critical and negative? But I must plead guilty. My expectations of him are probably more intense than they are for any other person in the world and, therefore, so are my disappointments. And, furthermore, I verbalize them freely to him.

As he does with me.

Some would say therein lies the danger of man/woman friendships; that surface kind of nonthreatening conversation can be so refreshing that it makes us hungry for more. It's such fun to act like we're wonderfully easy to get along with, when those we live with know we're really not.

When I have lunch with a man, I can listen with interest to new stories and jokes. (Larry and I have few *new* stories to share after almost fifty years.) I can overlook the too-strong cologne on a man I'll talk to for only an hour; I can't handle the pungency on someone with whom I share my life so intimately. So Larry hears me complain immediately and vociferously about any infraction of his that threatens my sense of comfort. Bob doesn't. Right or wrong, I can afford to be a little kinder to Bob, Fred, or Mike because I leave them promptly after lunch. They don't *have* to know my feelings and thoughts on so intimate and honest a level.

On the other hand, they don't get to know. To me, the intimate, honest sharing is a precious gift, though admittedly it rankles sometimes. If it's true that we can have as good a relationship with someone as we are honest with them, my relationship with Larry is bound to be a million times better than most just because of its honesty.

But it sure is fun to have a drink with Eddie after work now and then. Eddie sees me only as warm, fun, and happy. He's never seen the bitchy side of me. He doesn't know how picky I am when we look for motels on vacations. Larry could tell him how frustrating it is to hear me reject this motel because the room smells like cigars, and that one because the train goes right behind it, and the other one because it's under the flight pattern. By the time we find the perfect motel, Larry sighs, "Praise the Lord," and wonders why he chose *me*.

Eddie will always see me only as "easy to please." I have an image to uphold with him, and it's easy because our visits are so few and far between. I've no doubt that if Eddie and I were married, both of us would see entirely different people in each other than we see now. Of course it's fun to have a drink with him after work now and then; I get to act like I'm a joy to be with. That's how Larry gets to act over lunch with Nancy, Kathy, Rosemary, or any of the other women he enjoys seeing.

> Right or wrong, I can afford to be a little kinder to Bob, Fred, or Mike because I leave them promptly after lunch. They don't *have* to know my feelings and thoughts on so intimate and honest a level. On the other hand, they don't get to know.

As long as we're able to keep the opposite-sex relationships on a purely friendship level, there is no problem. What happens if we don't? Then we complicate our lives badly, as well as the lives of the other man or woman.

There was a man, many years ago, who was a close friend of the whole family. He was single, so he had lots of friends all over town, and he was a very loving person. Everyone who knew him loved him. Larry and I shared our problems with him as well as just doing things together that were fun. Both of us treasured him.

One day when he and I were chatting about love and marriage and commitments, he said something to me that I've never forgotten.

"Lee, you know how much I like you. I love you. There are times that I'd like to go to bed with you, but it would spoil everything."

"I know," I responded, and neither of us said anything more. Shortly after that he moved away, but I've always been so glad he said what he did. I delight in the memory of his warmth and honesty and affection. I even quote him now and then when people are considering having an affair. I, too, believe it would "spoil everything."

A married person can't cross that line from friendship and affection to sexual love without paying an enormous price. But there's nothing wrong with telling another person how you feel about him or her, as long as it doesn't lead to the next level of intimacy.

Addicted to Love?

Some people are unable to stop there. I have a good friend I'll call Kate. She's divorced and has had a couple of affairs with married men, which she now regrets. Kate confided to me that she no longer trusts herself when it comes to keeping a friendship simply a friendship.

"I can't afford to put myself in that vulnerable position again," she said. "I can have lunch with a married man if it's business or if it includes his wife, but I can't have the luxury of situations that might lead to romance."

She's probably very wise. Her track record is not a good one when it comes to backing away from married men. I have a lot of respect for her new intentions and I have no doubt she'll stick to them. She knows herself well . . . now.

"I still don't trust myself," Kate explains. "You don't get rid of addictions. You just learn to control them."

Is sex an addiction? There is a lot of debate about that question these days. Some people scoff angrily and say, "That's just a way to allow yourself to have affairs and not feel guilty. It's a cop out."

I agree that mankind has always found ways to excuse bad behavior. My friend John claims his affairs are because he's an Aries. "Aries always have affairs." Some men attribute their wanderings to their fathers, who taught them, "It's what men have to do. In Europe everybody has mistresses." People can always rationalize. "I require a lot of sex and my wife doesn't. It's a kindness to her that I go elsewhere for part of it."

While having affairs used to be more of a masculine trait, today's women are much less restrained than they used to be. I know a lot of married women who have cheated on their husbands and used variations on the same reasoning.

"I needed to find out what sex is like with other men. I was a virgin when I married, and I had to know how other men did it."

"Life was no fun anymore. It was either have an affair or a nervous breakdown. I think it kept me from getting a divorce."

And the classic, "I didn't mean for it to happen. It just did." (It's not my fault because I didn't plan it.)

Since time began, people have had sex with people when they weren't supposed to, but it's only recently that sex has been considered by some to be an addiction. There is no chemical dependency like there is in alcohol or drug abuse. But the alleged addiction stems from the temporary high one feels in the challenge, the chase, and the triumph. The feeling of high self-esteem comes strongly to those people when they've made another conquest.

If we define addiction as a habit that we can't seem to break in spite of the pain it causes ourselves and others, then sex would surely qualify. Many people have ruined their lives because of it, losing their spouses and families, and yet they continue down this path of destruction because of a burning "need" to prove themselves worthwhile.

Since we've already talked about the word "need," you know I don't believe it's a need at all, but rather a strong want. Either way it's a big motivator.

Addictions can also be positive. Dr. William Glasser says in his book *Positive Addictions* that it's good to have an interest that is so rewarding it becomes almost consuming.

Doing that particular activity restores us in some way, feeds us and rejuvenates us. We feel a sense of loss when we can't pursue that activity. Runners may feel let down if weather or illness prevents them from running. Artists feel they "need" to paint, and musicians look for bands in which they can "sit in" even when they're on vacation.

If we define addiction as a habit that we can't seem to break in spite of the pain it causes ourselves and others, then sex would surely qualify.

Perhaps any activity itself isn't good or bad, but our use of it can be. I saw a marriage break up over tennis, a sport we think of as a healthy activity. The husband was so driven by his desire to improve his tennis game that it took precedence over everything else in his life, including his wife.

The Twelve Steps

1. Admit you are powerless over compulsive sexual behavior and that your life has become unmanageable.
2. Come to believe that a power greater than yourself can restore you to sanity.
3. Make a decision to turn your will and your life over to the care of this higher power as you understand it. Combat the isolation you feel and belief that you alone have to solve your problems.
4. Make a searching and fearless moral inventory.
5. Admit to a higher power, to yourself, and to another person the exact nature of your wrongs.
6. Be entirely ready to have this higher power remove all these defects of character.

I believe almost anything can become an addiction. So I'm not uncomfortable with the term "sexual addiction" any more than I would be with "mudpie addiction."

The important thing is what we do about it. I applaud anyone who looks for ways to get back in control of his or her life. The twelve-step program that has been used to help millions of alcoholics, drug addicts, gamblers, and overeaters has been extremely successful. I can't recommend it enough to people with problems.

Most twelve-step programs include a daily recitation of the Serenity Prayer to remind everyone how to live their lives according to the twelve steps: "God grant me the serenity to accept the things I cannot change, courage to change the things I can, and wisdom to know the difference."

Those who feel they are addicted have found a sense of relief at finding a group of supporters who truly understand and share the problem. If you're struggling with the pain that comes from having

7. Humbly ask this power greater than yourself to remove your shortcomings.
8. Make a list of all persons you have harmed and become willing to make amends to them all.
9. Make direct amends to such people whenever possible, except when to do so would injure them or others.
10. Continue to take personal inventory, and when you are wrong, promptly admit it.
11. Seek through prayer and meditation to improve your conscious contact with a higher power as you understand it, praying for knowledge of your purpose and the power to carry it out.
12. Carry the message of recovery to other people in need and live your life according to the principles of The Twelve Steps.

a spouse who cheats on you, or if you're dealing with the pain that comes from cheating, I suggest you phone or write to the National Council on Sexual Addiction and Compulsivity (1090 Northchase Parkway, Suite 200, South Marietta, GA 30067; 770–989–9754) and find a local chapter.

Also, one of my friends has written a book that deals with sexual addictions. I suggest it to you for in-depth information by a professional who has had first-hand experience with a sexual addict she loves very much—and he, her. Together they've discovered Sex Anonymous and found it most helpful in understanding what they're trying to deal with. The book is titled *Back from Betrayal*, by Dr. Jennifer Schneider.

A No-Win Situation

Addiction or otherwise, the consensus is that affairs don't make anybody happy for long. They'll continue to tantalize us, appeal to us, and sometimes seduce us, but they won't be the source of lasting happiness.

That's not new information, of course. Almost all of us were taught that message by our rabbis, Sunday school teachers, priests, ministers, parents. I used to think "sin" was forbidden because God said so, and that God sat up there watching to see if we did something evil so he could zap punishment on us.

Now, I've come to believe that all the moral laws and ethical values we are taught over the years have been suggested not only by religious leaders, but by ordinary people like you and me who have tried these things and found them to cause pain. My friend Kendra McNally defines sin as "anything that's bad for me."

Sometimes it seems like we have to try out behavior for ourselves to see what the results will be. It's too bad we can't learn everything in life just by listening to or reading information handed down by "experts," but we don't. We keep reinventing the wheel, rediscovering that "If I do this, it's going to cause pain to somebody, including me." We keep taking risks and learning for ourselves what we can and can't get away with. In a larger sense, that's probably good.

How do we handle the hurt, though, that comes when someone we love is still experimenting with other people? Can we forgive infidelity? That deserves a chapter to itself.

What Does Faithfulness Mean to You?

As you've seen in this chapter, everyone defines faithfulness a little differently. Take a moment to each write out your own definitions, using the following questions as a guideline.

- Our marriage is (open, closed, somewhere in the middle) . . .
- I believe friendship with the opposite sex is desirable because . . .

  Or

- I believe friendship with the opposite sex is undesirable because . . .
- I think a wife and husband should have different boundaries in their friendships because . . .
- I think the same boundaries should apply to both husband and wife because . . .

continues

- My past relationships have altered my view of faithfulness and trust in the following ways . . .
- I get jealous of you and another woman/man when (e.g., you go out with this person alone, you flirt, you spend more time with this person than with me) . . .
- What do you see as the main reasons people are unfaithful (e.g., boredom, unhappy marriage, uncontrollable urges/addiction)?

10

Hard to Say
I'm Sorry

If I'd realized why I should do it, I might have forgiven people all along. Like so many of those other early teachings, "You must forgive one another" fell on my relatively deaf ears, except to make me mildly uncomfortable when I thought of all the people I didn't want to forgive.

I went for a whole year without speaking to my closest friend, Marie Magee, when we were in junior high. We walked the exact same path twice daily, nine blocks to and from school, on opposite sides of the street without acknowledging each other's presence. I really missed her, too, but I wouldn't consider forgiving her.

One day my mother called her over and "introduced" us and we giggled. We were friends again. Still, I never consciously "forgave" her. (Marie, if you read this, I forgive you. I just can't remember what I'm forgiving you for!)

Forgiving is one of the most difficult things to do. If we're hurt by someone, we have a tendency to keep that hurt alive and close to our hearts, even though it damages our relationship dramatically. Fanning the fire of hurt takes a lot of remembering, but we're good rememberers. Especially women. Men are better at forgiving because they forget. Women forget very little, so we have a harder time forgiving.

But men and women alike can hang onto old hurts tenaciously, almost cherishing them. Some of us get them out and look at them frequently, as we do with photo albums, keeping alive the pain we felt when Uncle Jerry ate our chocolate bunny when we were four years old, or whatever. Boy oh boy, we muse; that hurt! And can you believe Donna took away my date and kissed him at midnight at the New Year's Eve party? That was in 1949, and I remember it like it was yesterday. And in 1952, Mrs. White accused me of stealing stamps from the dormitory desk. Sure did hurt my feelings. In 1957, Larry called his folks but not mine when our second baby was born.

This is all from the woman who can't remember dates from history. Wars are unimportant, but my personal hurts? We're talking earthshakingly major!

I hate to admit it, but I'll bet I could jot down a lengthy list of remembered injustices that I have endured lo these many years. Have I forgiven them all? I like to think so, but the fact that I remember them so well makes me wonder.

But it's only been in the past few years that I've realized that forgiveness is for the forgiver's benefit rather than the forgivee's. Life is miserable for the hater. Have you ever been so angry with someone that you stiffened at the sight of his car or mention of his name? Your pleasant mood was absolutely ruined if that person happened onto the scene. And he could say nothing that didn't make you furious. I've experienced only one person like that, and that's all anyone needs in a lifetime.

> But it's only been in the past few years that I've realized that forgiveness is for the forgiver's benefit rather than the forgivee's. Life is miserable for the hater.

If he said, "It might rain today," it made me livid. I'm chagrined to admit the loathing I felt for him, and I felt totally helpless to change the situation. So I carried my evil secret around for years. Guess who was the miserable one? He appeared to be quite happy, actually, and that made me even madder. That one relationship taught me how hard it is to maintain an angry, resentful feeling for someone and endure the relentless discomfort that goes with hating.

I've heard that one person out of ten will not like me (or you either). So when someone shows signs of dislike, we can tell ourselves happily, "Oh good, that's the one out of ten. The next nine will, no doubt, think I'm delightful!"

In my defense, I was young. I like to think I've learned a lot since then. If faced with that same situation today, I'd have at least a dozen options I could pursue to resolve the problem. For starters, I'd simply tell him my feelings, using the good old "When you . . . I feel . . . because . . . " (See page 73.)

In those days I didn't know I had that right, so I kept the feelings deep inside me. Generally that's what causes hate—at least it encourages the process. The more we keep bottled up, the more hostile we feel, until we're like balloons ready to pop. It's a miserable feeling, and one we've all experienced.

Good Guys versus Bad Guys Mentality

My daughter Lisa says, "Our lives are shaped by those who love us and those who refuse to love us."

It's probably good for us to have folks around who refuse to love us because it calls on us to learn to cope. Naturally, we'd rather be surrounded by those who love us and believe in us and encourage us, and hopefully we have some of those. But we also learn a lot from the others. We can get tougher by being exposed to tough people. We can come to terms with the fact that there are some people who simply will never like us, let alone love us, and we can stand that.

I've heard that one person out of ten will not like me (or you either). So when someone shows signs of dislike, we can tell ourselves happily, "Oh good, that's the one out of ten. The next nine will, no doubt, think I'm delightful!"

Life is not easy. Some people dislike us. They hurt us, they reject us, and we suffer. No matter that *they* might be terribly unhappy themselves—look what they do to us.

Much of our unhappiness comes from being treated unfairly (in our eyes) by inconsiderate, insensitive, or just downright mean people. You may have seen the bumper sticker "Hell is other people." Each of us has our deeply imbedded set of "shoulds" about the way folks ought to treat each other, and they're constantly being violated. And yet most of us truly believe *we* are not the bad guys— *they* are.

Many times I have this experience in my counseling office. A woman comes in and describes her pain at living with a man who sounds totally uncaring. Often she cries as she talks. She doubts that anything will ever change in their relationship because this man thinks *she's* the one with the problem, and he's not about to conform to her wishes. She's desperate, angry, and depressed. As I listen, I have to agree that it would be tough living with that set of circumstances; and that if I were she, I'd feel as bad as she does. I empathize with her heartache and strongly urge that she ask her husband to come in, too.

"It would be so much more efficient," I explain. "If all three of us can get together, we can solve things more quickly than if you're the only one coming for counseling. Perhaps he'd come in for a session by himself so he could tell me how he sees things."

The fascinating thing is this: When he does come in, he turns out to be a good guy, too. As I listen to his view of the relationship, I hear the pain *he's* been experiencing. It's been rotten for him, as well. He's disappointed and demoralized and thoroughly discouraged; afraid to hope things will ever change because she's so sure she's right and he's wrong. He doesn't see it that way.

I feel the same understanding and compassion for him that I did for her, and I agree with a lot of what he says. The next step is for them to come together.

Often they've compared notes before they come back and are surprised to discover that I sympathized with them both. I accepted them both, even *liked* them both! Once in a while they're a bit hostile, each one hurt that I didn't find the other one to be wrong, faulty, flawed—the bad guy, the cause of the problem.

Truly, I've never met a "bad guy" yet. Often someone *sounds* bad when I hear the other's description, but later they make good sense when they explain their views.

I am convinced that most of us are good. We do not want to be mean or inconsiderate. We went into marriage in good faith, with every intention of loving this person forever and being a good spouse. But that doesn't take away the hurt we've suffered living with a mate who sees things so differently.

What needs to happen somewhere down the road is forgiveness.

Forgiveness Is for the Forgiver

Until I can forgive the person who's hurt me, I'm going to feel discomfort. When I say that to a client, I often see a setting of the jaw and a steely anger in the eyes. "Forgive?" they say incredulously. "I can *never* forgive. This person has hurt me too many times."

I understand. It may be way too soon to even consider forgiveness, and there's no rush. But it should be an eventual goal for our *own* sake, not the other person's.

When we're able to forgive, we feel immediate relief. The letting-go is dramatic. It's like a magic pill that makes a headache disappear instantly. It has a much greater impact on the forgiver than it ever can on the forgivee. Once again we're lightened; free to resume living without this giant burden weighing us down. And we did it all by ourselves!

It may have very little to do with the other person. He or she may not even know we've forgiven them. But we know, and that makes all the difference.

What holds us back, then? If forgiveness feels so all-fired great, why is it so hard to do?

Probably because we're scared. If we forgive, we might leave ourselves vulnerable again. As it is now, we've built this wall of resentment around ourselves, which we think keeps us safe from

If we forgive, we might leave ourselves vulnerable again. As it is now, we've built this wall of resentment around ourselves, which we think keeps us safe from hurt.

hurt. If we don't let other people get close anymore, we'll stay secure. Forgiveness would take away our shield and leave us frightfully exposed.

I am keenly aware of those feelings in myself. When I've been hurt in any way, I'm leery of that person for a while. Remember the old adage, "Hurt me once, shame on you. Hurt me twice, shame on me." Why would I ever put myself in a position to trust again so you can hurt me a second time, or third, or thirtieth, or two hundredth?

Well, we would be idiots to put ourselves in vulnerable positions time after time. For example, if I find that my friend Violet steals things, I'm not going to leave her alone with my jewelry box. That would be dumb. I can still like her, though.

If I've confided in Claudia and later find out that she divulged my secret to her book club, I've just learned not to confide in Claudia again. But I can forgive her and continue enjoying her as a friend. I don't have to hold a grudge or reject her, or tell everyone else how rotten Claudia is. I can just quietly decide to forgive. Even better, I can tell her my feelings. She might benefit from that information, and she would know me better.

"Claudia, when I found out you told the book club what I'd told you in confidence, I was really upset and angry with you. I thought you'd keep your promise not to tell. But I've had some time to adjust to it, and I forgive you. It won't stop our friendship, that's for sure."

Then, hopefully, I would let it go. Keeping that hurt alive benefits no one at all, certainly not me. The next time we met I could genuinely hug her with affection and go on with our relationship as if nothing had jarred it.

Admittedly, that's the ideal. Often I've not been able to forgive someone nearly that easily or quickly. In fact, more often than not it's been extremely difficult. But I see progress, and that's what's important. I see clearly how I want to act and feel. I get a little closer to that attitude each time I have to draw on my forgiving expertise.

Mostly I'm encouraged at finding that forgiving benefits me.

The Unforgivable

Let's assume you already knew that. You agree that holding grudges is a waste of time. You, too, want to let go and get back to loving. You're able to forgive friends and family with ease.

And then one day you discover your wife or husband has had an affair.

What do you do?

Naturally that's a heavy blow, one of the heaviest life deals out. Almost everyone feels enormous hurt, followed quickly by tremendous rage. So many feelings come into play. There is betrayal, shock, rejection, fear—indeed practically every negative feeling we're capable of experiencing.

The procedure at that point depends on your mate's intentions. Some wives or husbands having affairs are already on the way out of the marriage and have no intention or desire to get the marriage back into shape. They want a divorce. There might be little or no remorse because their hearts are already "married" to the new lover.

We'll deal with that in a later chapter. But many times the errant wife (or husband, but for now let's say it's the wife) is almost relieved to have been caught. She's embarrassed, ashamed, and sorry the whole thing happened. She explains how she got caught up in it, she apologizes, and she says, "Will you forgive me? I promise you it's over and I learned something from it; I love you more than I could love anyone else. I want it all behind us. It'll never happen again."

Now what do you do?

Maybe you believe her. You know her so well that you can read what's going on in her head. You know she's sorry, you know it's over and she loves you, not the other guy. You're glad she's back on the right track.

But it would be a rare person, indeed, who could say, "Sure, sweetie, I forgive you immediately and completely. From now on it's behind us. Let's just forget it. I love you, too."

That's asking an awful lot.

Wounded mates are usually so devastated at that point they wonder if they *ever* can forgive, and they *know* they can't forget. Their emotions are shot. They feel and act like accident victims in intensive care. Their spirits are bruised and beaten, and they ache all over.

They alternate between feelings of love and relief and feelings of anger and fear. They bounce back and forth. One moment they want to cry with joy and make passionate love. The next, they want to strike back and punish, causing hurt as they've been hurt.

They can think of nothing else. Their days and nights are filled with imagining scenes between the lovers. They hunger for details of it, and they feel sickened at thinking about it. There is almost no peace of mind. They're haunted by the fear that maybe the other person was a better lover and now nothing will ever be good enough. They're defeated, inflamed, and enraged.

Forgive? They wouldn't know how to begin, even if they wanted to. The hurt is too intense.

The mate who cheated is usually repentant at first, wanting only to be forgiven and have the marriage "back to normal." It's the mate who was cheated on who is not willing to drop the issue yet— sometimes not for a long, long time. It seems to be the only topic of conversation in that household. Nothing else is important anymore.

A typical conversation between a husband and wife who's found out about his affair might go like this:

> **She:** More coffee?
> **He:** No thanks. It was a great dinner, honey.
> **She:** As good as *her* dinners were?
> **He:** Oh, please, do we have to talk about that again?
> **She:** What do you expect? I find out you're in love with another woman and I'm supposed to act like it never happened? It *did* happen, damn it. How do I know it isn't still going on?
> **He:** Because I've told you it's over, and I mean it. I don't know what else I can say. It's over, that's all. How long do we have to keep hashing it over?

She: As long as it takes, that's how long. Until I can believe in you again. I trusted you and you broke that trust. I can't just pretend it never happened. All day long when you're at work, I wonder if you're calling her or if she's calling you. I can't work anymore. All day long I think about you and her. And you expect me not to talk about it? I can't believe you!

He: Honey, it's over. It's a dead issue. I learned something. I'm not about to let it happen again . . . ever. All I can do is promise you I won't call her. I won't talk to her even if she calls me.

She: She is calling you, then?

He: No! She isn't . . . she won't. She knows it's over.

She: How does she know? Have you been talking to her?

He: (sighing) No, not since the day you found out. I called her and told her it was over and I wouldn't see or talk to her anymore. And she shouldn't try to contact me, either. I told you that.

She: And you expect me to believe you after what you've done?

He: Look, I feel totally helpless. I tell you the truth and you don't believe me, anyway. Why do we keep talking about it? It doesn't get us anywhere.

She: Because I'm so profoundly hurt, that's why. You don't seem to realize what you've done to me—to us. I'm not sure I can ever forget it.

The conversation goes on and on in the same vein, getting no place, leaving both parties frustrated and discouraged.

But it's easy to understand both sides. She *can't* trust him. He *can't* seem to reassure her. They're stuck in a miserable place.

Setting Limits

I generally suggest that they do need to talk about it, but it might be helpful to limit the conversations on this subject to so many minutes a day. I might say, "It would be almost impossible for Karen *not* to talk about the affair. She's too scared and too hurt. But you're right, Mike, that going over and over it isn't doing either of you any good. How about you both determine how much time every day you want to discuss it and limit this topic to only that much time, say, twenty minutes a day at first. Every day for twenty minutes Karen can talk about it, ask you questions, tell you off, describe her fears and her feelings, ask for reassurance, for twenty minutes straight.

"Then, when the time is up, the subject is closed for the day. You're free to talk about other things, go someplace, do something fun. It would be great if you put some fun back into your lives. You've suffered enough, you two. How about taking dancing lessons, going to basketball games, or having a dinner party?"

Mike is tickled to death with my suggestion, because twenty minutes a day sounds like heaven compared to the relentless pursuit of the subject up to now. Karen is generally reluctant to agree to this. "I can't just shut it off the rest of the day," she says.

"You can *think* about it if you want," I tell her. "You might even want to write in a journal. Put down all your feelings; write out your anger and define your fears. It'll be an interesting book to share with someone going through the same thing someday, if you ever feel like it. It might help them so that they'll get over it eventually."

Karen agrees, with some misgivings, and we make another appointment. Usually they report that it helped, when they return the next week. Often Mike is saying, "I think we could cut down to ten minutes a day," and Karen rejects that idea. For her it's been extremely hard to stop at twenty minutes, and understandably so. She sees this as a dangerous and insidious disease that's attacked their marriage. She's frightened out of her wits that history will repeat itself, that she'll never again be able to relax and trust like she did before.

She doesn't *want* to let it go at this point. She wants just the opposite—to make life so miserable for him that he'll never, ever let himself even consider cheating again.

In addition to the very normal fears she's experiencing, she probably wants a little revenge on him for messing up her life so horribly. She still has a need to punish him.

Is she wrong? Probably not. But is it doing her any good? Also, probably not. Certainly she has a right to her hurt and anger, and she also has the right and the responsibility to tell him her feelings.

But at some point it becomes nonproductive. There's no new information being traded, no new insights to help with understanding and empathy. It's all been said. To continue discussing it only belabors the issue and flogs the dead horse.

> Once we have the desire to let anger go, we can begin to do it, even if we take tiny baby steps.

The long-punished guilty person begins getting resentful of the relentless punishing from the innocent one. "He deserves every bit of discomfort he feels," many people would say. Hell hath no fury as a woman scorned—or a man, either.

Forgiveness Is a Decision

Sometimes I ask, "How long do you want to stay angry with this person?"

The answer is usually a puzzled, "Well, how do I know?"

"Well," I suggest, "what would be the length of time you'd recommend to your best friend? How long should someone else stay angry for this same kind of offense? A month? A year? Three years? Forever?"

Frequently, the person thinks about it and says, "I don't want to stay angry at all, I really don't. I just can't seem to let it go. I'm scared to relax, I think. I'm afraid to trust again. I can't help it."

I understand those fears. The important thing is that now there is at least a tiny desire to get back to normal. "I don't want to stay angry at all" is a healthy step. Once we have the desire to let anger go, we can begin to do it, even if we take tiny baby steps.

I have total faith in anyone's ability to achieve forgiveness once they decide that's what they want to do. The decision is a giant step in itself.

Perhaps the word "forgive" means something like "I don't want to stay angry at all" or "I'd like to be able to let it go." Forgiving doesn't mean condoning bad behavior. Often we're reluctant to forgive for fear it will imply we think the behavior was OK after all. But that's not what it means, not at all.

What does it mean, then?

One possibility is the saying, "Hate the sin but love the sinner." I can disapprove strongly of something you might have done, but I can love you just as dearly as if you'd never done it at all.

To me that's been easiest to do with our children. Parental love is so strong that most of us are easily able to forgive our children for practically anything, especially if they admit to making a mistake and are sorry about it. It's harder with adults who are not our flesh and blood.

Love Is a Decision

So, perhaps it's the love that enables us to forgive, more than the circumstances or logic involved. If I love you, I'm going to want to forgive you much sooner than if I didn't love you.

"I did love her," said one cheated-on husband, "but she killed that love when she slept with that other guy. I can't love her anymore."

That's not an unusual feeling, but it needn't continue if the man wants to love again. You've probably seen the posters that say, "Love is not a feeling but a decision." Sometimes we need to decide, consciously, that we want to love, in order to open ourselves up for the feelings we once knew as "love." To act in a loving way, even if we don't feel like it, can actually increase our love for our mate, and our mate is quite likely to respond.

What if a mate is not very loveable? If we wait for him to act loveably, it might take a long, long time, but we don't have to wait. We can start loving even if the other person isn't ready. We get to love anytime, and we can love anyone. That's a privilege no one can take from us.

I need only to decide I want to love you and then begin to act as if I already do. Have you noticed how many movie actors fall in love with their costars? Over the years there have been quite a few. I suspect the "acting in love" makes the process happen in fact.

We get to play movie star! I know I'm oversimplifying, but I truly believe we can set upon any course of action we choose, and our feelings will follow. Feelings follow action.

Give your energy to anger and punishment and your feelings will stay stuck there. Focus the energy on loving or acting as if you're loving, and you'll fall in love before long at all.

The choice is ours. And our enjoyment of life will be determined largely by the choice we make. If I choose to stay angry, keep the hurt alive, punish, reject, and process the injustice someone has done over and over and over, I'm going to keep myself miserable.

If I choose to want to forgive, let go of the whole thing, act as if I love, and keep my energy active on "loving the sinner," I'm going to be a whole lot happier.

It hasn't got much to do with the other person. I am the one choosing my behavior. The way I act and think will determine my state of mind. I would hope always to opt for the forgiving stance, rather than harboring resentment.

> Feelings follow action. Give your energy to anger and punishment and your feelings will stay stuck there. Focus the energy on loving or acting as if you're loving, and you'll fall in love before long at all.

Repeat Offenders

What if I forgive and love again, and then he has another affair and hurts me again? A valid question and one worth considering. We have to decide for ourselves how many of those we're willing to tolerate. Some will say, "One. After that the marriage is over."

I'm not sure how I feel because I've never had to face that problem in my own marriage. I know legally I'd have no problem divorcing an unfaithful husband. Even morally it would be understood by my church. Society would understand and probably condone divorce under that circumstance.

But it's nice to know I get to make that decision regardless of anyone else's principles or rules. I might choose to forgive a couple of times, I don't know. I think it would depend on how repentant my husband was, and how much I value the marriage.

I know some men who would die before they would ever be unfaithful, but in other ways they're jerks. Staying faithful doth not necessarily a good husband (or wife) make. Anyone can make a mistake, even two or three mistakes, and still be a gem.

Guilt Is a Decision

I think sometimes we make too much of infidelity, setting it up as "the unforgivable sin," when maybe it needn't be. Interestingly, my experience has been that a woman will forgive a husband's cheating far more often than a man will forgive a wife's. I don't know why.

Women feel just as devastated and shattered as men do at the discovery of an affair, but in my observations, they've been more willing to let the pain go and try harder to work on the marriage. Men have usually seemed so angered, they're ready to junk the marriage on the spot.

But one can't generalize, I know. Every person decides what he or she would do if their spouse had an affair. I can't tell you what's right for you.

I know what I would want to do, and that's to forgive this wrong just as I've forgiven all the others. But please understand that I'm not condoning infidelity. Nor do I condone lying, stealing, or even cheating on history tests. However, I've done all three. Although I've regretted doing them, I learned something important: They caused me more unhappiness than happiness.

Most of us have done many things that go against our moral belief system. Yet, at the time, we seemed to find justification for them. Often it's been after the fact that we find the reasons we shouldn't have done them.

Sometimes we know full well we shouldn't be doing whatever it is we're going to do, yet we do it anyway. I smile at the statement

Lisa made one day when she was excitedly planning a trip to an expensive resort in Sedona that she couldn't afford. "There is no justification to my spending that kind of money," she admitted, "so I won't even try to justify it. I'll just do it."

We all do things we can't justify. If we learn from them, they're probably good for us, unless they've hurt someone else in the process. When we do hurt someone, either accidentally or deliberately, we need to apologize and make restitution to that person if possible.

Then we need to forgive ourselves.

That's difficult, too. Sometimes we hang onto guilt long after it's necessary. A little healthy guilt is good for us, and I disagree with those who say it's needless. If I hurt you, I should feel guilty!

But what I do with guilt is the important thing. If I use it to remind me that other people are not to be trifled with, not to be disrespected without discomfort on both sides, it's a healthy reminder. If I use it as impetus to try to make restitution, it's positive. If I use it as fuel to keep myself miserable, it's unhealthy. And sometimes we do just that. We go over and over in our minds some incident that we regret, keeping ourselves in a continuous snit of regret and remorse, kicking ourselves when we're down, punishing ourselves relentlessly to absolutely no avail.

> Most of us have done many things that go against our moral belief system. Yet, at the time, we seemed to find justification for them.

It's useless behavior. What's done is done. Sometimes we fall victim to a state called *scrupulosity*, in which we are excessive in our self-punishment.

I once had a client who married quite young, and she and her husband had used recreational drugs pretty foolishly. In one of her mind-altered states, she'd slept with a friend of his, and at the time it seemed the OK thing to do. But as she got older and smarter, she looked back at that incident with a lot of regret.

It became an obsession with her. She stewed about it constantly, even dreaming about it at night. She confessed it to her rabbi, her father, her mother, and finally her husband. She saw one

> Usually, the reason we hold onto guilt is for the false sense of "goodness" it gives us.

or two counselors before she came to me. All of us told her virtually the same thing. "It's over. It was wrong, but you saw that and quit the drugs that led you into it. It can be forgotten, now."

Easy for us to say. She couldn't forget it. She believed that God loved her, understood and forgave her, but she still wouldn't forgive herself.

When we flat can't (or won't) forgive ourselves, we need to look for the payoff we're getting for keeping that unnecessary guilt alive. That kind of guilt is neurotic guilt—a useless, crippling state that does us way more harm than good.

Usually, the reason we hold onto guilt is for the false sense of "goodness" it gives us. Our unconscious rationale is something like this: "I must be a very, very, very good person to feel this guilty this long. My pain and suffering prove how noble and worthy I am. This intense discomfort makes me morally superior to those who might do wrong and promptly forgive themselves. I refuse to forgive myself in order to elevate myself above the rest."

Now, of course, that's not thought out at a conscious level. In fact, people who get into that state of unrelenting guilt see themselves as distinctly unworthy. But frequently, if they can see that they're holding onto the guilt to make themselves feel "very, very, very good," they might become willing to let it go and join the rest of us ordinary people who do dumb things and feel guilty but finally forgive ourselves.

We need to forgive—ourselves and others. There's a line in the Lord's Prayer that says, "Forgive us our trespasses as we forgive others." What if it said, "Forgive us our trespasses as much as (and no more than) we forgive others?" Or "as much as and no more than we forgive ourselves." I wonder if that would be more of an incentive to forgive.

Again, religion and mental health go hand in hand, as they so often do. Whether we look at forgiveness as something taught by our spiritual leaders, or as an attitude that's going to make us feel better, we're going to be happier people when we forgive than when we don't.

Practice Forgiveness

Practice forgiving by starting small, with past hurts you haven't been able to let go of. Think of all the harm holding a grudge has caused *you*. How much harm has your grudge caused the one who wronged you? Picture yourself free of that grudge and the uncomfortable feelings that go with it. Visualize rising above it. If you still can't seem to shake it, ask yourself what you get out of holding on to the grudge. A feeling of superiority, martyrdom? Protection against getting hurt? Has it really worked?

——11——

Baby Love

Many young people today have decided not to have children, and some couples who do want them find they're unable to conceive. Many of you may have already raised your children and you're not interested in information about that part of your life anymore. You folks might want to skip the next two chapters, both of which address the subject of how children affect marriage.

First of all, I will establish this crucial fact: Having four children and helping them grow up to be happy, healthy adults is the most meaningful achievement in my whole life. Nothing else means as much.

The entire wall space on both sides of our hallway is filled with pictures: Laurie and Lisa on one wall, Lindsay and Lyle on the other. I like to stand in the hall brushing my teeth and gaze at them in maternal adoration. I treasure each child and offer God a fervent thank you for them at least once a day.

But . . . it was a big job.

As every parent knows, the time and energy needed to rear a child boggles the mind. Are they worth it? They are to me. Should everyone have children? I sure don't think so, any more than I think everyone should get married.

But when we are parents, it's really helpful to learn some things that will make the job easier. Most of us graduate from school, find work, marry our prince or princess, and have our first babies without ever having a class on parenting. It would never occur to us that we need one. We assume parenting comes naturally, if we ever think about it at all.

When we do think about it, it's usually in lovely fantasies. On starry nights with the boy or girl of our dreams, we revel in imagining the wonder of how it would be.

> **We assume parenting comes naturally, if we ever think about it at all.**

"If we get married, would you want children?"

"Of course. A little girl just like you."

"And I want a boy like you. Oh, won't they be cute? Maybe we should have four or five. I love kids, don't you?"

"Sure, they're neat."

On one of those starry nights, Larry and I took it a step further by suggesting, "Wouldn't it be fun if we all had names that start with 'L'?" I wiggled with the joy of it all. And so we did what we set out to do. In fact, after naming Laurie, Lisa, Lindsay, and Lyle, we acquired pets: We named the dogs London, Lovey, and Licorice. Our cats were Lasagne and Leilani.

But finally I got tired of so many L's. One week before Christmas, I brought home a darling puppy who needed a name. I thought, "No more L's! Maybe a Christmas carol name?"

And then I thought of "Noel."

No "L."

And so she was our token "no L" for some fourteen years. The point being that sometimes what you dream of does come true—just in time for you and your dreams to change!

Every year we take pictures for Christmas cards, with the entire family looking rested, happy, and as though there's nothing we'd rather be doing than posing together. People may even think we always look that way.

I hereby publicly admit we don't. (But by now the Christmas card picture is a tradition that can't be dropped because all the cards are framed in the hall next to the girls' and boys' pictures.)

But what did Larry and I know when we brought the first baby home from the hospital? Zilch. Nada. We didn't know a whole lot more when we brought home the second, third, or even the fourth.

Now we're experts, as are most grandparents. By the time we no longer need the skills, we've got them down pat. How did we learn? By making jillions of mistakes.

Fortunately there are lots of books on parenting these days. Almost every women's magazine has an article on parenting. (I wonder why they seem to be lacking in men's magazines.) Parenting classes are available at community centers, schools, churches. Such classes are particularly helpful because parents get to hear other parents talk about their problems and find out they're not alone. All parents struggle to do the best they can.

But a book on marriage wouldn't be complete without a chapter on the joys and trials of parenthood. After all, now that I'm an expert, I want to use my skills a little bit!

In the Beginning

It starts out pretty easily. The days of feeling queasy and tired are all part of the excitement to a first-time mother. It's such fun telling everybody, "We're going to have a baby!" that both the woman and the man feel a nice importance, like they've done something pretty special. Indeed they have. There's nothing more special than a human life.

Sharing the experience of the birth is one of the most profound occasions a couple will ever have. Usually they feel very close during those first few days in the hospital.

When they take the baby home, they're thrilled beyond words. And the excitement is compounded by friends and family coming by with gifts and good wishes, and everyone agreeing that the baby is the marvel of the century.

The next few months, however, are some of the toughest they'll ever face. Unless the baby is highly unusual, he or she cries a goodly amount and seems to need hours and hours of care. According to a pediatrician I know, the care requires seven hours a day. How do you find seven extra hours every day?

You give up any free time you might have had before. Pretty soon you begin to get tired and cranky. You feel like you haven't had a full night's sleep in years, though it's been only weeks. There's a sinking fear that life may never be the same again. Both parents feel haggard; both believe they need and deserve a little time for themselves.

They get testy with each other. At times they're even resentful of the baby, which causes them to feel guilty and think they must be awful people.

Sex

For the most part sex goes out the window for a while, partly due to the woman's physical condition, but even more because of her emotional indifference to sex. It's not permanent, but the husband begins to think it is. The more frustrated he becomes, the more resentful he is.

The new mother is enchanted with the sensual feeling of the baby's skin against hers. She had no idea it would be so heady a relationship. The innate love she feels toward the newborn child finds her totally unprepared. She knew she'd love her baby, but she hadn't an inkling of how much.

> I emphasize that this turned-off state is temporary. The danger comes only if one or both parties fear it will be this way from now on, because fear exacerbates the problem.

Neither did her husband. He feels more than a bit miffed at her endless cuddling and sometimes grows weary of the baby being their only topic of conversation these days. While sex might have been equally important to both before, it's a rare wife who continues feeling erotic at the same level after she gives birth.

Again, I emphasize that this turned-off state is temporary. The danger comes only if one or both parties fear it will be this way from now on, because fear exacerbates the problem.

As the husband watches his wife's love affair with the baby, he feels distinctly unimportant to her. He may or may not express his threatened feelings, but those very natural feelings of rejection will probably surface in some way. She'll feel the disapproval in his manner and become uncomfortable about it. She knows exactly what's causing it, but she feels helpless to try to change. So intense is her feeling of responsibility for this new person in her life that it seems unthinkable to focus less attention on the baby.

Nevertheless, she knows she has a certain responsibility toward her husband, too, and so sometimes sex becomes "a duty." She wants to be a good wife. She does love her husband. So she may initiate sex some nights even though she's exhausted and longing for sleep. Perhaps it's not terribly rewarding to either of them. That causes them to worry about it even more.

My best advice for young parents is this: As much as you can, convince yourselves that this is only a temporary setback in the sexual arena. The only thing you have to fear is fear itself, because that fear becomes the real deterrent by mushrooming into a Giant Problem.

It doesn't have to.

When you know what to expect, you handle it much more easily than when you don't. For instance, knowing that children will lose their baby teeth makes that process one we take in stride. If we *didn't* know it was normal, we might feel tremendous concern. "How will my child be able to chew?"

It's that same unnecessary fright that young parents endure over the question of sex. "Will we never again feel the passion and desire we've always had before?"

If you know it's a passing phase that everyone else has survived, you can see it as a minor irritant, but nothing to get in a snit over. Libido returns, as do teeth. Trust the process.

However, if the sexual relationship does *not* return after a few

However, if the sexual relationship does *not* return after a few months, you'll know there's some other problem to deal with. One or both partners may be choking off a normal desire for sex because of reasons that have little or nothing to do with the new baby.

months, you'll know there's some other problem to deal with. One or both partners may be choking off a normal desire for sex because of reasons that have little or nothing to do with the new baby. The problem may be pent-up, unresolved anger. It's virtually impossible to experience anger and sexual desire at the same time, so we have to resolve the hostility before the desire can return.

In fact, it's easy to blame the birth of a baby for the deterioration of a relationship, but it's not usually the baby's fault. If the relationship suffers any major setbacks, they're more likely caused by a lack of communication. When we keep sharing respectfully with each other, all feelings should proceed in a nice healthy way, including sexual ones.

Still, the warm, romantic interludes are generally quite diminished for a few weeks or months. That fact along with the seemingly constant demands of the infant can put a real strain on the relationship.

I suppose it would be lessened if one could afford a Mary Poppins–like nanny who would tend to the needs of the wee one, freeing the parents to go off by themselves and have fun without worrying about the kid. But most of us can't afford that lifestyle.

You should try to get breaks when you can, though. Asking a neighbor or friend to baby-sit is good sense. Children are happier when their parents love each other, so you do them a big favor by having fun yourselves. You're definitely not uncaring parents when you get a trusted sitter and go out for a few hours. On the contrary, you're adding to your store of mental health, which will benefit rather than harm the baby.

Beyond Baby

But even without a child to complicate our lives, there is usually a gradual lessening of the intensity of sex. Indeed, marriage itself often marks a certain reduction in sexuality between two people who used to be extremely sexual together. You may have heard that the best method of birth control is marriage, because you quit having sex. It's a joke, but there's a certain amount of truth in it. Forbidden fruit is always the most appealing, and once it's there for us in abundance, it often loses some of its attractiveness.

A couple who are truly committed to each other and the principle of marriage needn't worry that their love lives are down the drain just because there are children added.

> Children are happier when their parents love each other, so you do them a big favor by having fun yourselves.

Communication with lots of honesty and respect should clear the way for genuine warmth and love, including plenty of romantic love. Both people need to feel perfectly free to express all their feelings, even the "bad" ones. Remember, feelings are never right or wrong.

It's perfectly appropriate to say, "I feel resentful of how much time the baby takes."

Or, "I miss the days when it was just you and me alone together."

"I feel like second fiddle. All your love seems to be directed at the baby." Or, "I'm hurt that you don't seem to love the baby as much as I thought you would."

"I don't always want to be the one who feeds her in the night."

"It feels like our romantic days are over, and I'm scared to death."

"You seem disinterested in me and the baby."

"It makes me mad that you refuse to change a diaper."

Expressing our feelings helps us feel better, but there's no guarantee that we'll get new behavior right away. Still, having expressed ourselves, we know we've planted a seed of information that might sprout into a positive change later on.

And even if we never get results, we're happier letting our feelings be known than hiding them and pretending everything's fine. That is the sure-fire killer of sexual desire!

Communication with No Strings Attached

To feel understood is such a precious gift, and one we can give each other even when we can't immediately solve a problem. Our tendency is often to jump in and defend ourselves or argue about the other person's feelings. We want to say, "You shouldn't feel that way!"

Reminding ourselves that feelings are not right or wrong might help us accept them in ourselves as well as in the other person. The immediate need is not so much to find a solution as it is to share some feelings and understand each other.

Let's use this statement as an example: "I miss the days when it was just you and me alone together."

Some possible responses guaranteed to cause trouble:

"You jerk! You think you should be the center of the universe all the time, don't you? Well, you're going to have to share me for a long time, so you'd better get used to it."

Or, "Yeah, well, everybody has to grow up sometime."

"You shouldn't feel that way! You should love the baby and be glad we have him!"

"You sound like a selfish little kid."

"Then why did you agree that we should have a family in the first place?"

"You think I like it?"

The understanding response would allow the feelings, accept them, and also express your own:

"I know. It was nice when it was just the two of us, wasn't it? But this is nice in a different way, to me. The baby will need less time, little by little. I hope you know I still love you!"

Why is it so hard to respond that way? We love each other. We love the baby. We want to be kind. And yet, so often, we lash out in an attacking kind of response.

Acknowledging Fear

An attack of any kind comes from someone who feels afraid or victimized. It's easy to empathize with the fear both parents feel.

Usually, the new mother is so captivated by her new role that she's threatened at the thought of having to "give up her love affair." Any criticism from her husband sets off alarms in her head that she might be asked to change her focus back to him.

From his viewpoint, of course, there's fear that he's lost his friend, lover, and playmate. She's so different now. So from that vantage point of fright, both partners act out in anger, pouting, withdrawing or distancing.

It helps so much to know that unloving behavior is almost invariably coming from the position of fear. It makes it so much more tolerable and nonthreatening. I can understand and love you and feel compassion for you when I know your bad behavior stems from fear. I hope you can react the same in the face of my bad behavior. To reassure the fear often takes care of the disrespect.

> It helps so much to know that unloving behavior is almost invariably coming from the position of fear.

But all of us can spout wise sayings and preach mentally healthy responses when we're calm, comfortable, relaxed, rested, and unpressured. We're *never* in that state when we have a new baby around the house! So, we're vulnerable to overreacting, getting our feelings hurt, feeling victimized, and wanting revenge. It goes with the territory. We wouldn't want it that way, but it happens. Again, it's like the flu. We get it and we get over it, and we're happier when we're able not to give it too much importance in our lives.

The tiredness and apprehension that come with the baby go away. We get to keep the good part—that marvel of the century!

12

We Are Family

Marriages are often troubled by differences in beliefs about how children should be handled. A frequent complaint I hear is this:

> My wife is so permissive, she's ruining our kids. She lets them run all over her. They are completely spoiled, and she can't control them. When I'm alone with them, they behave just fine, but the minute she comes in the door, they start fighting or whining or getting in trouble, somehow. They're constantly demanding things. It's gotten so I hate to go home, there's such turmoil there. She complains how exhausted they make her, but she doesn't discipline them. They abuse her, and she puts up with it. It's going to ruin our marriage.

You can imagine that the father, in his frustration, begins to overreact in the other direction. He becomes the stern, hostile parent because he knows the kids need to be taught discipline and he thinks he has to balance his wife's permissiveness.

Parenting Then and Now

Let's look at a bit of history to see how these differences in our belief systems have come about: Parenting wasn't nearly as confusing in the "olden days." Parents didn't worry much about children's feelings. Rules such as "Children should be seen and not heard" were widely held, and physical punishment was the norm. Kids knew where they stood. Father was the head of the house, and the words "Wait till your father gets home" struck terror into little misbehaving hearts.

There were kind fathers, of course, as well as kind mothers, but one thing was believed by parents and children alike: Parents were the bosses and children were submissive. If you knew what was good for you, you didn't make waves.

And it worked. By and large, kids minded parents. Today it's a whole different world. Why? Back in the days of yore when there were powerful people running the world, kings lorded it over the "lesser folk." They made rules like, "If you disobey our laws you get your head chopped off," and the poor peons knew they meant business. After seeing a few of their friends lose their heads, the ordinary folk wisely minded the rules.

But there were always a few brave souls willing to risk their lives, and now and then they would revolt. There was always a revolution someplace, and many of them were fights for equality. It took hundreds of years for human rights to become a rather common issue, and for most of those years men stayed "superior" to women. Everybody knew their place.

Father was the chief boss, followed by subservient mother, and kids were the peons with no rights at all. The system worked up until World War II, when women had to (or got to) go out in droves to work in war plants and such. Rosie the Riveter changed things for good.

Women came back to tend the home fires when the war was over, but they no longer believed that their husbands were more important than they. They felt "just as good" after their exposure to the outside world. And most of them got downright cocky and dared to challenge men's supremacy.

Whether men believed women were equal to them didn't matter; the women believed it and acted accordingly. No longer willing to "mind" their husbands blindly, they began to do things to prove their own importance.

My own father looked askance at wives who worked outside the home. When my mother decided she was going to work anyway, he was not pleased. But they needed the money; their teenage children were self-reliant; and, of course, Mama agreed that she'd still cook a grand dinner every night and the housework wouldn't suffer. Off she went to an office for eight hours a day. Dad could see that things were no longer the same, and he reluctantly accepted the changes.

My mom was one of many thousands. She was influenced by other wives who were declaring their independence, and they encouraged one another. They got to enjoy the heady feeling of earning money, which gave them some power in decision-making that they'd never before enjoyed. Some men still resented it, but they began to see they were fighting a losing battle. No longer would women feel or act as though they were of lesser importance.

That was the revolution that ended men's superiority, but there was still a major revolution to come—the children's. Little boys and girls all over the country watched as Mom became "as good as" Dad. They watched equality raise its head, and they couldn't help but like the idea!

They began their own revolt with the belief, "If Mom is as good as Dad, then I'm just as good as them both!" Whether Mom and Dad agreed was unimportant, the fact was already established in the children's minds. No longer were they willing to be submissive and subservient. Just as men had struggled against women's rebellion, parents now struggled against their children's emerging strength, but it was too great a force to be held off.

Society was now completely withdrawing from the old-fashioned autocratic system. Some of us might wish it were still in existence, but it's gone and we can't wish it back.

What does that mean, then? Surely as parents we still have the right to make the rules and see that our laws are carried out.

> Little boys and girls all over the country watched as Mom became "as good as" Dad. They watched equality raise its head, and they couldn't help but like the idea!

We'll "chop off their heads" if they disobey! We'll punish them, by God. And we may, but in our children's minds is the strong belief, "If you have the right to punish us, we have the right to punish you," and you may already know how good they are at this.

> The most autocratic, powerful, punishing parents are surely rearing the most rebellious, powerful, punishing children.

The harder we punish them, the more ways they can find to get back at us. Though punishment can often be effective with very young children, it loses all effectiveness as they grow older. In fact, it will have served only to demonstrate that power gives us permission to "lord it over" others. The most autocratic, powerful, punishing parents are surely rearing the most rebellious, powerful, punishing children.

If we're smart, then, we have to find other ways to teach our children. Certainly we can't relinquish our responsibility and let them do as they please. But gone are the days when reward and punishment were the best teachers, if they ever were.

Too Much of a Good Thing

Fortunately there are wonderful skills that are easy to learn and so much more effective than the old punishing ways. Today's children who are lucky enough to get the benefit of the newer methods of discipline will almost certainly grow up to be more responsible than if they'd been "punished into submission."

They'll also grow up mentally healthy. In the olden days, mental health was not necessarily the norm. People did conform, yes, but inwardly they did a lot of unhealthy resenting and rebelling in insidious ways. They weren't honest and respectful with each other. They lived illusions of being happy families, but there was a great amount of unhappiness in their lives, too.

Disrespect was the order of business in the olden days. The process of life was finding one's place in the hierarchy and living accordingly, even if it violated human rights.

It's marvelous that we've come so far in our awareness that people shouldn't be mistreated. Society needed that realization. But when parents bought the concept of respecting children, they sometimes went overboard in the other direction.

They swung from being tough, controlling, punishing, autocratic parents to being wimpy, overprotective, and permissive, which was no doubt worse. The one good thing about autocratic systems is that at least there is some sense of order, with everyone knowing his limits.

There is probably *nothing* good about the permissive system. All it does is teach children that the world is there to serve them. Children of permissive parents don't learn self-discipline or responsibility. They become greedy and selfish and unable to deal with the real world. They are dependent on others and resentful of those on whom they depend. All in all they're the most abused of any children, because they're deprived of learning their own sense of self-reliance and the value of work and discipline. Work is worth. We need to have work in order to feel good about ourselves, whether we're astronauts or three-year-olds dusting the piano.

> Children of permissive parents don't learn self-discipline or responsibility. They become greedy and selfish and unable to deal with the real world.

Permissive parents have the best of intentions, raising children with "love." But unless their love includes discipline and responsibility, it's not very loving. When children are given whatever they want, they come to believe that's how life should be, which is a sadly distorted view of the universe. In permissive homes, children are the tyrants who rule, and parents are the lowly peons, there only to serve.

A Happy Medium

All right, so what do we do? We don't want the old autocratic ways anymore, which taught disrespect by punishing and produced rebellious young adults who were determined to control and humiliate as they'd been controlled and humiliated. Nor do we want permissive homes that produce weak, demanding tyrants who collapse when faced with the challenges of real life.

We want, instead, strong children who grow up to be responsible and healthy, physically, mentally, and emotionally. We want them to be able to make good decisions in all the facets of their life: work, family, and society. We want them to pull their own weight, not being merely "takers" who lean on others. We want them to learn assertiveness and develop the confidence to go after what they want, respecting their own needs as well as everyone else's.

In order to become that kind of adult, they have to learn early in their lives how to *make decisions.* The only way to develop good decision-making expertise is to make decisions, whether good or bad.

So the kind of home we want for our children's best possible development is a democratic one, in which there is honesty and respect, and plenty of opportunity to make decisions. We want our children to decide all kinds of things for themselves, learning values as they go.

Decision-Making Formula

As a rule of thumb, I like the Out of Eighteen decision-making formula, in which you let a two-year-old make two decisions out of every eighteen, a nine-year-old make nine decisions out of every eighteen, and so on.

Assume that in a typical morning there are roughly eighteen choices that affect your two-year-old's life. He gets to make two of them and you make the rest. At age two he's capable of deciding whether he wants to wear his green sweater or his red sweater out to play. You decide whether or not he needs a sweater at all, but he gets to choose which one. You decide to serve juice for breakfast, but he may choose between apple and orange juice. You decide when he takes his nap, but he may choose which animal he takes to bed with him.

By making those decisions at an early age, he's already on the road to making bigger decisions. So at nine years old he's capable of making nine out of eighteen, or half, of his decisions.

By then he's such a pro at choosing options, we can enjoy the pride we feel at watching his good judgement. How did he get so good? By making nine thousand dumb decisions in his early years and having to live with the consequences. When he makes a choice and he's not happy with the result, he's just learned something useful—not to make that same choice next time.

A child who gets to make so many of his own decisions gets skilled at it, so that by age eighteen, he's perfectly capable of making eighteen out of eighteen decisions. In other words, all of them.

If we've done our job well, we can watch our eighteen-year-olds graduate from high school and feel confident in their ability to go out in the world and live productive lives. That's really what all of us want for our children.

But out of our mistaken beliefs, we often cripple them with overprotection. We rescue them from their bad choices, we remind and nag, and we virtually live their lives for them, so that at age eighteen they're no more equipped to handle life than they were at age two.

> We rescue them from their bad choices, we remind and nag, and we virtually live their lives for them, so that at age eighteen they're no more equipped to handle life than they were at age two.

And then we shake our heads with worry and say, "This kid has no sense at all. She's simply not a responsible person. And after all we've done for her!"

Those of you with children under two have a great advantage. But even if your children are older, it's never too late to initiate this process. They'll still be way ahead of children who never get the benefit of learning responsible decision-making.

A word of warning, however: It's hard to do. Because we love these children so much, we hate to see them hurting in any way. Our empathy for them is so fine-tuned and our compassion for their discomfort so strong that it takes all the restraint we've got to keep from rescuing them. We know so well what's good for them, and we

Breakfast:
A Decision-Making Example

My friend and mentor Dr. Oscar Christensen uses the example of an ordinary breakfast as a setting for teaching. I offer his illustration:

> I would not give a two-year-old the decision as to whether to play with my shotgun or not. But I might be so bold as to allow a choice of cereal in the morning, whether it be Crispy Critters or Cheerios—he decides.
>
> As you probably guessed, the traditional mother would have given the youngster oatmeal in the first place because she knows that is best. After three bites of oatmeal, the child refuses to finish. Then begins the process of reward and punishment, the traditional approach for making the child eat. Mother begins with bribery.
>
> "Honey bunch, this is yummy stuff; now eat this gruel; it is good for you. You'll love it. Eat this and you can have some toast with sugar on it." "Eat this and I'll give you a dime." "Eat this or I'll hit you." That is the full routine for an autocratic approach. Finally, the last punishment: "Okay, bad kid, down from the table."
>
> Now, on the other extreme, the permissive mother would give the child two bites of oatmeal, two bites of cereal, two bites of egg, two bites of anything else he wants and finally at 11:30 she would get disgusted and send him from the table and wonder why he didn't eat lunch.
>
> The mother we are trying to create is the one who says, "You decide, Crispy Critters or Cheerios?" But once the milk is poured, the decision is irreversible. You can't recrisp a soggy critter. This is his breakfast and this is the decision the child has to live with. If any

of you have dallied over your prepared cereals in the morning, you will recall that within a very short period of time they can become worse than the oatmeal in appearance and texture. Therefore, I would make a fairly safe prediction that if he doesn't stick to his decision and immediately eat his cereal, this youngster too would come to the same conclusion that his breakfast is not edible.

At this time, mother would give him his second choice of the morning, "Either eat the cereal or excuse yourself; you decide." Now chances are the youngster will jump down from the table in glee because he didn't have to eat the cereal. At that point, mother may say, "I see you have decided to excuse yourself."

Those of you with any experience at all know that at 10:00 both of the youngsters are going to be back; they are both going to be hungry; they are both going to be nasty to live with. The oatmeal non-eater comes back to mother and says, "Okay, you dumb old mother you, I am hungry and it's your fault. It's your fault. You sent me from the table." Unfortunately, there's just enough truth in the statement that mother typically feels guilty and gives him forty graham crackers before sending him out to play.

When the child who excused himself comes back at 10:00 to complain of his hunger, his mother says, "Yes, I'll bet you are. It's probably because you didn't finish your breakfast this morning. Maybe tomorrow you will. Now run along and play; I'll see you at lunch."

Regardless of how the mother handled the situation, it is my contention that both children learned. There is no such thing as a nonlearning child. Both children learned. The oatmeal non-eater learned he can do anything he wants to do so long as he demonstrates that it is someone else's fault.

want to protect them from any pain they might encounter when they make mistakes.

So we teach them exactly what they should do in every situation. Then we remind them over and over. In case they didn't hear us the first time, we make sure to remind them a third time, a twenty-ninth, and a sixty-third.

We take responsibility for their lives, doing them a dreadful disservice. How much more loving we are when we respect them enough to let them make choices, knowing they're smart and that they'll learn from good and bad choices alike.

The Overprotective Parent

One of our biggest temptations is to rescue our children from the consequences of their choices. Sometimes I think if we all switched kids and raised each other's we wouldn't get so tuned in on rescuing, because we have a better sense of perspective with other children. Our own are too precious to us. We too often refuse to allow them to experience any discomfort at all, even if it's healthy for them.

I confess to having been one of the most overprotective mothers in the world. When counselors pointed out the harm I was inflicting on our children, I was disbelieving at first, but I finally came to see they were right. That was the first time I realized we can't always trust "common sense."

If you're not sure just when you "overprotect" or "rescue," an example of my own overprotective days may help. In second grade, Laurie played often with our little neighbor, Debbie. One September afternoon, they were playing in our backyard when suddenly I heard raised voices, then tears. Laurie raced into the kitchen wailing that she and Debbie had found an autumn leaf in our backyard and had reached for it at the same time. Debbie maintained she'd seen it first, so it should be hers; Laurie claimed ownership on the grounds it was in her yard. They'd fought over it, and Debbie had taken the leaf and run home. Laurie was clearly expecting me to do something about this dreadful happening. And I came through (I hate to admit) in my best "Supermom" style.

I phoned Debbie's mother and said sweetly, "We have a problem." I explained the whole episode and waited for *her* to solve it just as Laurie had waited for me. Sure enough, she too came through.

"Well," she said thoughtfully, "maybe it would be a good idea if they split the leaf and each took half."

I pronounced it an excellent idea, suggested it to Laurie, and she met Debbie halfway down the block, where they divided the leaf.

Debbie's mother and I congratulated ourselves on a job well done.

What a shame I deprived Laurie of finding her own solution! Not that it did any lasting harm to her little psyche, but I missed a golden opportunity to help her become more confident.

If I had it to do over, I would say, "I can see how upset you are, Laurie. Let's talk about it. What do you think you might do?" Giving her a chance to explore the possibilities for herself would have been much more respectful.

She might have said, "I could never speak to Debbie again."

"That's certainly one option," I'd have agreed.

"I could go take a leaf from Debbie's yard."

"You could do that."

"I could tell Debbie's mother on her."

"Yes, you could."

"I could go find another leaf in our yard."

"There are probably quite a few there," I might agree. Finally, when she'd thought up all her options, I would have asked, "Of all those choices, which do you think you might try?"

"Telling her mother."

"And what do you think her mother might do or say?" We would discuss possibilities and I would end the discussion with, "You're really good at finding lots of solutions, Laurie! I'm eager to hear what you decide to do and how it all comes out. Keep me posted."

That would have been respectful to all concerned. Instead I "stunted her growth" by moving in at once with a ready-made solution. And that's just one example out of hundreds I look back on and regret. I solved and suggested and rescued four kids several times a day for years and years. It's amazing they turned out so well in spite of me.

I would have been the first to argue with anybody who said I wasn't respecting my children in the days when I overprotected. I *thought* I was being a terrific mother, but actually I was only indulging myself in feeling so necessary to them.

Fostering Self-Reliance

Every time we do something for a child that she could do for herself, we diminish her a little. We rob her of the pleasure of accomplishment and pride she can enjoy as she builds her self-esteem.

In our defense, we do it with the best intentions. We get so used to doing things for them, we don't think of how much they can do for themselves.

When Lisa was in kindergarten, I picked her up with her friend Erin and went to visit Erin's mother. Erin asked Lisa, "Do you want some toast?"

Lisa nodded agreeably, and I watched with amazement as Erin dragged a chair to the kitchen counter and put bread into the toaster. It had never occurred to me that five-year-olds could make toast! I probably would have continued making my children's toast till they were thirty-five years old, but for that insightful day. Erin had three older brothers, so her mother had already discovered that kids can do all kinds of things.

Most of us do things for our children that are totally unnecessary. I recommend to clients that they let their children start doing their own laundry at age eight. They often look as surprised as I would have, had anyone suggested that to me when my kids were young.

> I solved and suggested and rescued four kids several times a day for years and years. It's amazing they turned out so well in spite of me.

We overlook the fact that today's children can quickly learn how to operate VCRs and computers. Certainly washers and dryers are a lot simpler.

We can begin preparing them when they're five or six. "Sweetie, when you're eight you'll get to do your own laundry!" We say it with the same excitement we'd use in telling them, "When you get a little older, you can go visit Grandma and Grandpa all by yourself." And on their eighth birthday, we teach them how to work the washer. We count on some mistakes, but we can anticipate what those might be. So we teach them not to overload, and we explain sorting light and dark colors.

Larry and I used to be head residents in a college men's dormitory. Every September there would be knocks on our door from disturbed young men holding pink shirts and shorts. "Mrs. Schnebly, I washed my clothes and my red socks must have faded on my white stuff. What do I do now?" The poor dears had been deprived of that information at age eight and now had to learn the hard way.

We can do our children a real service by helping them become capable and self-sufficient from the earliest possible age. While that also frees us parents to spend more time pursuing our own interests, we're often uncomfortable with it. Mothers, especially, get a great deal of satisfaction from being needed, and also from nurturing. Sometimes there is even an unrealized anxiety that our children might not "need" us. Or we may fear their disapproval. We're so vulnerable to their expressions of sadness or fear or anger that we're putty in their hands.

I don't for a moment accuse them of consciously manipulating us, but unconsciously they come to know what they can get away with. Later on in life they often look back and see clearly how they manipulated us. They laugh and shake their heads at how creatively they got their needs and wants met.

But can we, as parents, see the dynamics as clearly while they're happening? I don't think we can because we're too emotionally involved. We see the mistakes easily in *other* families, however. We see a child "abuse" a parent in the supermarket, begging for candy or toys, crying, having temper tantrums, and we see the embarrassed parent writhe in a no-win situation. If the father yells at the tot or slaps him for misbehaving, he risks the disapproval of us observers. If he gives in and buys the child the candy or toy, he still risks the disapproval of us observers.

The kid knows he has Dad over a barrel. That would probably never happen if we had a neighbor's child at the market. Both the neighbor's kid and we would have more respect for one another than to let that situation occur.

If the child said, "Can I have a candy bar?" our response would be a kind, firm, "No." We would see things clearly. Candy is not good for this child and it will not become an issue.

Our enormous love for our own children makes us want them to enjoy pain-free living, which seems to translate into never being deprived. It's as if love clouds respect. I can easily refuse the neighbor's kid whom I *don't* love because I'm clear about what he can or can't "stand." We respect the neighbor kid's ability to handle a candyless tummy. Our own little angels make us doubt their ability to handle *anything* displeasing to them.

> Our enormous love for our own children makes us want them to enjoy pain-free living, which seems to translate into never being deprived. It's as if love clouds respect.

Again, I don't want to sound like I see children as crafty, cunning, selfish individuals who are out to get us. But I do see them as incredibly brilliant in getting their wants met. God gave all of us an innate ability to figure out how to survive, and a precious gift it is! The smarter we are, the better we're able to use that gift to help us get what we want.

It helps to look at our children's manipulative techniques as evidence of their natural intelligence. Instead of being annoyed with them, we can be genuinely grateful they're so smart and capable of figuring things out. Once we think along those lines, we'll be able to react logically, instead of emotionally, to their behavior.

Encourage Your Children, Encourage Each Other

The truth is, encouragement may be the greatest gift we can give our children *and our spouses.* Encouragement helps us all thrive and bloom. Children need encouragement like plants need water, and they wilt drastically when they're deprived of it.

We adults don't really *need* it as we did when we were youngsters, but it enhances our lives immeasurably. To encourage, we let others know 1) we deem them important in our lives; 2) we value them as human beings; 3) we believe in their ability to succeed at whatever they attempt.

Furthermore, we want to *sell* them on all three of these beliefs. Unfortunately, even when parents do see their children in these ways, we neglect to let them know. The same is true of our interaction with one another.

And yet we, as individuals, have tremendous power with which to influence every member of our families. Each time any two get together, both walk away either more turned on or more turned off.

Every one of us has the potential to affect others' lives positively or negatively, and yet too often it doesn't occur to us to do either one. Not that we'd *want* to affect someone negatively as a rule, but sometimes we do when we're angry. To make a person feel more positive about him- or herself is a skill we could use a dozen times a day at least. And that's all encouragement is.

It can be verbal, of course, complimenting them on something you genuinely admire. To your eight-year-old, "Sweetie, I love the way you help your little brother that way. You sure have a knack for seeing what people need!"

To a spouse, "When I get to the kitchen first thing in the morning and find the paper already in and waiting for me, I really admire again how thoughtful you are."

Or, "You're so good at telling jokes! And I'm always so proud when I see everyone at the party laughing at them!"

To a teen, "We know we're lucky parents when we see another great report card like this. You've always worked hard in school, and it shows."

To a first-grader, "I love watching you play with your friends in the backyard. You seem to know how to include all of them in whatever you're playing."

To a mother-in-law, "I'm a lucky woman to get to enjoy the fruits of your labor in raising this man we both love!"

To a ten-year-old struggling with his homework, "Alan, you've been working so hard on that math assignment! You really have stick-to-it-iveness!"

But encouragement doesn't have to be verbal. It can come through body language, like a wink as you pass the mashed potatoes. A pat on the shoulder as you walk through the room where your daughter's watching TV lets her know, "I like seeing you."

Certainly a hug or kiss communicates affection that can be a big part of encouragement.

And asking advice is a gem with both spouse and kids. "Which should I buy for our garden, petunias or pansies?" It's saying, "I value your opinions. You have good taste."

"Which tablecloth should I use for dinner when the Bromiels come over?" A five-year-old or a forty-year-old can answer that and feel your trust.

Any comments or questions that show our respect for an individual act as encouragement. We value them and we want them to know it. A fringe benefit is that the more we recognize their goodness, the less we have to deal with their badness.

> Any comments or questions that show our respect for an individual act as encouragement. We value them and we want them to know it.

One of our most successful businessman friends admits, "I'd go through fire for a pat on the back." All of us hunger for positive reinforcement.

Recognizing any positive behavior is a sure way to make it continue.

When Not to Encourage

Unfortunately, recognizing any negative behavior can be a sure way to make *that* continue. We want to be unimpressed with behavior we want to discourage.

Being unimpressed is slightly different from ignoring. To ignore something, we have to pretend it isn't happening. To be unimpressed, we can be aware of it but just not respond to it. We treat it the way we would an airplane flying over. We may notice it, but we don't pay any special attention to it.

When we quit paying attention to certain behaviors our children exhibit, however, an interesting thing may happen. They may begin to think we don't love them anymore. Sometimes their claim to fame has been so wrapped up in getting attention for a certain activity that they mistake our withdrawal for disinterest. Frequently they will increase the bad behavior, trying harder and harder to get us involved, and they become even more discouraged when they get no results.

So, while we should turn our attention away from misbehavior—which includes anything we don't want to happen, from acting wild to excessive shyness, persistent fears, refusing to join in, pouting or brooding—it's extremely important to give extra attention for other things at the same time. This is the time to lavish encouragement on the child for anything at all that's positive.

No Such Thing as a Perfect Parent

Children often enjoy experimenting with their behavior, seeing how far they can go with each parent, with grandparents or sitters. They love a sense of power just as adults do. They'll exercise their power in whatever way they're most successful. The best child, the best-at-being-the-worst child, the most outgoing, the shyest, the healthiest, the sickest, the happiest, the saddest, "our little worrier," "our helper," are all tried-and-true roles.

And all children delight in getting their parents involved with them, whatever it takes. Indeed, they often cooperate to get their parents' attention by fighting with each other.

When things are a bit dull, one or the other will deliberately provoke a scene. Even the tiniest tot learns to knock over his big brother's blocks so big brother will wail and perhaps

> And all children delight in getting their parents involved with them, whatever it takes. Indeed, they often cooperate to get their parents' attention by fighting with each other.

clobber the baby as both of them yell and begin their mental countdown: ten, nine, eight, seven, six, five, four, three, two, one . . . here comes Mommy!

Sure enough, there she is, coming in from the kitchen, looking disturbed and saying, "Now what is it?" The kids are tickled pink. It worked again!

They've just seen once more that the best way to get attention from Mom is to stage a fight. Even if the attention consists of a lecture or punishment, it's well worth the price to experience that sense of power at getting adults involved.

We should be thrilled with their persistence, even while we determine to defeat their negative methods. We should beam proudly and think, "What fertile little minds they have!" But we'll remember not to get hooked into their game of "Getting Parents Involved."

So we look for ways to encourage their self-reliance. "I notice you two solved your own quarrel. You're getting really good at that! I'm impressed. How about playing a game with me, anybody want to?"

Ideally we'd keep in mind pictures of how we want our children to be as adults, and all our behavior would be working toward that image. Are we fostering their ability to entertain themselves? Are we teaching them our values? Do we rescue them or let them experience the consequences of their actions? Do we respect them? Do we respect ourselves? Do we communicate feelings, thoughts, ideas, and ordinary day-to-day stories of incidents? Do we show love? How loving are we as wife and husband, and are there signs of affection between us that demonstrate that love to them?

What if we fail in any of these areas? We do and we will, but that's okay, too, because it's modeling the realities of life. Few of us grew up in homes where the atmosphere was ideal. It might be safe to say that most of us grew up in families where people didn't express their true feelings. There was deceit and disrespect, or criticism instead of encouragement. Throughout all of it, the family members put on a show of normalcy that they knew didn't exist.

But that's all right. It didn't kill us, and we always have the opportunity to learn new ideas and beliefs and behavior as we grow up. Certainly it would be a lot easier to grow up in a home where there is always respect, honesty, communication, affection, and encouragement. But when there isn't, we can either be defeated by it or we can grow from it—we decide.

So, if we make mistakes as parents, we needn't spend much time harboring our regrets. Don't say, "If only." Say, "Next time." Indeed, if we were perfect parents, perhaps our children would be cheated out of the opportunity to learn from our mistakes. And though we'd prefer not being unfair or disrespectful, our kids may become a little tougher by experiencing some unfair treatment now and then.

There are always going to be teachers, neighbors, bosses, friends, and spouses who treat them unfairly. Life is not fair. Perhaps they would be too tender and vulnerable if they had never experienced that at home.

So we mustn't be too hard on ourselves for our imperfections in parenting. Let's chalk them up as reminders that people are prone to making mistakes; our children are entitled to make them as well.

It's wonderful when we can readily admit our mistakes to our children. To prove that we have all the answers is not necessary. To show we're always seeking to learn is exemplary. To apologize to them for our angry outbursts or other behavior we regret is marvelous modeling. We don't have to always be right. We can say, "I don't know," and "Maybe I'm wrong." We can ask our four-year-olds or our teenagers, "What do you think?"

As parents we needn't be perfect, thank goodness, but we do have to be the family leaders. We're not here to fulfill their every need or desire. We're the camp directors, trying to help our charges learn, grow, and expand their horizons.

> It's wonderful when we can readily admit our mistakes to our children. To prove that we have all the answers is not necessary. To show we're always seeking to learn is exemplary.

Parenting Styles

Sometimes it seems that being a good parent can get in the way of being a good partner. Take a moment to discuss these different relationships and how they affect each other. Following are some questions to get you started.

On a scale of 1 to 10, with 10 being overprotective and 1 being authoritarian, how would you rate your parenting style?

> **My style (wife):**
> **My style (husband):**

How would you rate each other's style?

> **My husband's style:**
> **My wife's style:**

How do the differences (or similarities) in your styles cause conflict in your marriage? Think, for example, of the last time you disagreed about how to handle your child's behavior.

How would implementing the Out of Eighteen decision-making formula (see page 162) affect your child's behavior? How would it affect how you treat each other?

When was the last time you encouraged your child (or children)?

When was the last time you encouraged each other?

13

Please Don't Talk about Me

In-laws. The very word sounds ominous. More jokes have been told about in-laws than almost anybody else. (Someone once said that we laugh at the things we're afraid of!)

I could almost entitle this chapter "Fear" because that's what it's all about. To realize that many of our problems stem from fear is encouraging. Knowing that takes some of the sting out of the pain and gives us a direction toward which to work: alleviating fear rather than building walls of protection.

I wonder how many wars have been fought out of fear, and how many could have been avoided if the people involved had been able to talk about their fears instead of becoming enemies?

What Are We So Afraid Of?

Alfred Adler taught that man's greatest need is the need to belong. We all hunger for the security of being loved and accepted and thought worthwhile. Most of us have always felt that acceptance in our original families, but it is threatened when we branch out and start new families.

We're astonished when the dreaded in-law syndrome settles on us because we never thought of ourselves as mean or selfish or controlling or rigid or domineering or any of the nasty words associated with in-laws. We're caring and thoughtful and considerate! To know us is to love us. Everybody *else* likes us. How is it that only the new mother-in-law, father-in-law, son-in-law, or daughter-in-law objects to us? We feel victimized, thrown into a role we didn't want.

> We fear change. We fear the unknown. We fear not being loved and accepted for who we are. We fear being expected to love someone we don't know very well, yet.

Most of us rooted for Romeo and Juliet and loathed their closed-minded families for trying to prevent their marriage. Our hearts went out to Maria and Tony in *West Side Story* as they fought against the prejudices of their extended families. We are a culture that believes in falling in love and choosing our lifelong partners ourselves.

And so everyone says sensible things such as "Whomever my children choose for their spouses I will love. I want only for them to be happy." And everyone means it. What goes wrong, then? Why is there so much pain involved with the families we marry?

Fear.

We fear change. We fear the unknown. We fear not being loved and accepted for who we are. We fear being expected to love someone we don't know very well, yet. What if they aren't the kind of people we're drawn to? What if they have entirely different beliefs? What if they alienate this treasured loved one of mine and I lose him or her forever?

Both sides are sharing the same fears. When we fear anything, we tend to want to escape from it. That's an innate protective habit. Run. Avoid. Shut out.

And in the case of in-laws, that's the direct opposite of what we should do.

We can become so terrified we lose all confidence and begin to act differently around "The Person" than we do around anyone else. We're frozen into a false kind of manner, a kind of phony smile through teeth clenched in fright, trying to act as if we're comfortable when inside we're scared to death.

If one of us would say, "I'm scared of you," maybe the other would make the same admission, because that's basically all that's wrong with any of us.

We can understand fear because we've experienced it in so many other areas. Perhaps we've learned to handle our fear of flying, dogs, heights, or snakes, but we haven't been able to practice dealing with any fear until we find ourselves in the thick of it—cornered, sweating, and feeling helpless.

As a little girl I picked up on the strained relationship between my mother and her mother-in-law. It seemed to me that Grandma just didn't like Mama. My interpretation was that mothers-in-law were to be feared, because if they didn't like you, you were in for a life of trouble.

When I married Larry, I approached my in-laws with trepidation. I laugh now when I remember writing them a letter and copying it three times to ensure that it was perfect so they wouldn't disapprove of me. Years later when I confessed that to Lucille, my mother-in-law, she looked astonished and amused and said, almost disbelieving, "You *did?*"

She knew I had nothing to fear from her, but I'd been aware of their discomfort about Larry marrying a Catholic. (It's funny to look back at how many times religions have gotten traded back and forth. God must be amused watching the big flap it causes sometimes, when in the next generation everybody is going to be switching again. I doubt that God gets too concerned.)

But I came to be very fond of my mother-in-law and she of me. Over the years I watched various friends and relatives struggle with their new in-laws. I would puzzle over all the resentments and hostilities. In spite of my own relationship, I began to see in-law discomfort as the norm rather than the exception.

And it continues. Almost every week in my counseling office I hear statements from tense clients:

> "My mother-in-law wanted her son to marry someone with a college degree. She didn't approve of me because I was a waitress. It took years before she accepted me."

"I told my son-in-law that if he ever so much as makes my daughter cry, I'm going to tear him limb from limb. She's still my little girl and I have to protect her."

"My daughter-in-law forbids me to give my grandchildren even one cookie. She believes sugar is bad for them, and I can't have the pleasure of seeing them enjoy my cookies." (The counterpart: "My daughter-in-law stuffs my grandchild with sweets and I can hardly stand it. It's all I can do to keep my mouth shut.")

"My father-in-law lords it over us with money. He buys us things—TV sets and even cars—and I resent it. He acts like I can't support his daughter. I don't want his money, and I wish he'd butt out of our life."

In every comment runs a common thread: Fear. Everyone's afraid of changes they're expected to make, of having to give up behavior or values that are important and precious to them. We're scared of not being loved anymore, of being rejected, or of just not feeling like we belong.

It would be lovely if we didn't have to endure this strained stage. Some few lucky ducks escape it, usually when they've known each other for a long time and have had time to get used to each other. But the majority of us seem to experience it for some period of time, perhaps like an initiation.

It helps to know that this strain is common; we're not the only ones enduring it. Most of us get over it. We simply have to know that there are tried-and-true ways to handle fear of any kind.

What Can We Do about It?

Do the thing you fear to do. If you're afraid of heights, you have to go over bridges. Afraid to fly? Take some airplane trips. Dogs? Get one for a pet.

The problem only worsens when we back away from what we fear, yet that is our tendency. The more we distance ourselves, the more afraid and estranged we become.

New sons-in-law don't seem to have as much anxiety as new daughters-in-law. That's probably because women tend to be more emotional and more tuned in to one another's feelings. To women, close family relationships are more important than they seem to be to men. So the bride and her mother-in-law generally experience some wariness in meeting each other.

> Ideally, all the in-laws would be best served by going into the new lifestyle with confidence and trust, believing they'll get along just fine.

Just knowing that in advance helps quite a bit. It's almost a universal truth, so it helps both people to recognize the fear they share. This recognition is a common bond right from the start, which makes it less fearsome, doesn't it?

Daughters-in-law, keep in mind that what your mother-in-law wants most is for her son to be happy. And she'll love you to pieces if she sees him that way. There may be some who feel jealous if their sons love another woman besides Mom, and if that's the case, we can be quite sure she has some serious problems. Of course, the son can help the situation by letting Mom know he still loves her. Sometimes I think those sons have the biggest challenge of all, making two women feel loved!

Ideally, all the in-laws would be best served by going into the new lifestyle with confidence and trust, believing they'll get along just fine. Then, if there's trouble, they can deal with it as it comes along, but they don't have to dread something that might not be a problem at all.

Miscommunication

When our son Lyle met Ginger, we were eager to meet her because we could tell she was special to him. We got to join them for brunch and were delighted with her openness and sense of humor. She was the picture of confidence and easiness, and we couldn't help seeing how well they "matched."

We weren't surprised when Lyle confided that he thought they might get married someday. I told him honestly I thought they had a genuinely good relationship.

In just a few months, however, they were setting a wedding date. Then I began to feel apprehensive. It seemed to me they were rushing into a decision that was too important to make so quickly. One day, when we were having a lighthearted lunch, I told them my thoughts.

"I know I'm biased," I admitted, "because I spend so much of every day hearing stories of married people who are unhappy. Most of them thought they were perfectly suited to each other, but now after some years together, they have lots of problems stemming from the differences they are now able to see.

"I think you two are rushing into this," I continued, "and I feel like I have to tell you my feelings. But if you still go ahead with your plans, I promise I'll support you a hundred percent. I'm not trying to talk you out of marrying . . . only into waiting a little longer."

Both Lyle and Ginger looked receptive and composed and as friendly and warm as ever, but I'd shaken Ginger to the core. From then on our relationship changed. She drew back in hurt, feeling I was rejecting her, and I drew back in fear that now I had alienated them for good.

We still interacted, but there was a sense of apprehension and anxiety that made family festivities hardly festive. Birthdays and special occasions that used to be full of warmth and laughter were now feeble attempts at trying to act as though we were having a good time, when underneath we all felt the strain.

Ginger felt uncomfortable and confided in Lyle. I felt uncomfortable and confided in Lyle. Lyle was in the worst position of all, loving all the people involved, yet helpless to foster any sense of genuine warmth among us.

But we proceeded diligently, perhaps courageously, with the wedding plans. Both families seemed to enjoy the actual wedding and reception; and I really think we all did, because we had decided to. It was going to happen, and we wanted it to be happy and special for the bride and groom.

All of us hoped that somehow down the road, things would smooth out. And we knew that we had one strong thread in common—we loved Lyle. We wanted to be comfortable and close to one another.

One day I decided to make an audio tape, because I felt I could tell Ginger what I was thinking in a slow, safe, carefully thought-out way. I sat down one morning and talked to her the most honestly I ever had, describing my fears, hurts, and hopes, all into my safe little tape-recorder microphone. I shed a tear here and there, and it was therapeutic for me to get all of those thoughts expressed. I dropped the tape at their house for them to listen to at their leisure. It seemed to help immeasurably. They listened to it together, and Lyle called to say thanks. Ginger wrote me a note saying she thought we could forget the past hurts and start all over, because she wanted to as much as I did.

Lyle and Ginger were married for four years before she decided to end the marriage. In that time we'd become far more comfortable with each other, and it was too bad we couldn't have foreseen that comfort factor in those painful early months.

On the other hand, if the future had been predictable, they probably wouldn't have married. Ginger found she wanted a husband with qualities different from Lyle's, and within a few months of that decision, the marriage was over.

When In-Laws Become Exes

Our daughter Lisa had a similar experience when her first husband, Paul, realized he missed dating other women. They'd been married just two and a half years when he confided that fact first in me and then in Lisa, who had had a miscarriage just a few days before.

They'd had several sessions with counselors, but Paul's heart was not into marriage improvement. He was frightened by the responsibility of fatherhood, and losing the baby gave him a window of opportunity through which to be young and carefree again. He knew then that he hadn't been mature enough for marriage, and Lisa could see it was futile trying to hold on.

There's no question that it hurt Larry and me to watch two of our children go through divorces they hadn't wanted. It's what parents often fear in the first place: seeing their child's pain caused by a marriage gone sour. We may try to help them see potential problems before they commit, but that advice generally falls on deaf ears.

> **Like everything else they do as adults, marriage is one of the risks children must take themselves, win or lose.**

Like everything else they do as adults, marriage is one of the risks children must take themselves, win or lose. Parents have done their jobs by then and can do little but share their thoughts and feelings with their children. Then they'd better let go of our concerns as much as they're able and focus, instead, on being supportive of the couple as they try to make it work.

If they can't make it work, their parents should continue to be supportive by listening and loving. It's good to suggest counseling, as one might to anyone who's struggling through difficult times. And to remember that marriage difficulties are not the end of the world.

Lisa now revels in the joy she shares with her husband Tom. "I learned a lot from that first marriage and from all my experiences with men," she confides. "I came to realize what qualities were important to me, and I was so much better able to recognize them by the time I met Tom." She treasures him and their daughter and son, Sedona and Rye, and knows by comparison what a good match this one is.

Lyle, too, has a wife who's perfect for him. Both he and Cheri have had previous spouses, and they seem very appreciative of the commonality and comfort they've found now. This time I couldn't have chosen better if I'd wanted to, they're so well matched.

No Such Thing as the Perfect Match

Being "well-matched" is not always as important as some other factors in choosing a mate. Parents would like to see the important similarities present to make the newlyweds' lives simpler: both coming from the same race, same religion, same socioeconomic background, same education. Our friend Fred says in jest, "I think my mom would have even preferred I marry a guy, she wanted everything so much the same!"

Young people find those differences much less important. To them, "being in love" is all that matters. In fact, sometimes the differences make the attraction even more exciting.

Seventeen years ago, when Laurie married Pete I had a lot of fears. It seemed like no two people could have been so different from each other. Pete was street smart, had run away from home many times, served time in jail, ridden the rails, used and dealt drugs, got into street demonstrations in the Sixties and, as Laurie said in admiration, "He has scars all over his body!"

Laurie was Miss Patty Perfect—sheltered, cautious, an honor student who read books for entertainment. I was very concerned about their chances of a long, happy marriage, and I know Pete sensed it in me. One day Laurie reassured me that it was perfectly okay if Pete and I weren't crazy about each other, and she told him the same thing. Her understanding and permission were comforting.

He and I were always courteous with each other, but there was a bit of a strain. Finally we talked about it and agreed we had similar guarded feelings, but I could honestly tell him I was glad Laurie had married him because they obviously loved each other a lot.

It was a worthwhile discussion, with both of us agreeing to be more honest with the other and not walk on eggshells in each other's presence. We ended the talk with a hug, and as we walked down the hall together, Pete said, "Lee, I'm glad I'm not married to you. You'd drive me crazy."

It was spontaneous and funny, and I laughed genuinely as I assured him it went both ways. I wish we'd been as direct before, because it relieved the strain we'd felt.

On the flip side, what can seem like a perfect match may not be after all. When Lindsay introduced us to Barb, there was an immediate "click" of rightness, and all the Schneblys thoroughly enjoyed watching the romance blossom. Witnessing their wedding, I felt a wonderful awareness that now all four of our children had lifetime mates they could love as they grew old together. It felt marvelous!

And it was marvelous for eight years. But as I write this, I'm sad to report their impending divorce. A year ago Barb told Lindsay that she wasn't happy being married anymore. She wished she were still single so she'd be free to go out with other men.

She agreed to go to marriage counseling with him, but she made it clear in the first few sessions that she simply wanted freedom. Lindsay continued the therapy alone, and it's helped him immensely, but it's been the toughest year he's ever experienced. Assured by Barb that he'd done nothing wrong didn't seem to help much because he kept searching for reasons that he couldn't find.

Fortunately, he had a lot of friends and family for support, and we're all sure he'll find someone else down the road. Who knows, maybe they'll be a better team than he and Barb were.

But three out of four of our children have been or are about to be divorced. That from parents with a forty-nine-year marriage, a solid spiritual life—and a mother who's a marriage counselor.

It happens, that's all.

And I readily admit that I think the present spouses are far more suited to my kids than the first ones were. In Lindsay's case, the results are still not in, but I've no doubt his next wife will fit that description as well.

Will We Ever See Our In-Laws as Family?

No marriage is problem-free. But when the commitment is present, and the desire to communicate is strong, the chances of success are excellent. By the same token, no in-law relationship is problem-free, but it's fun to feel the intimacy develop as we spend time with each other and share experiences. Every family vacation, indeed every shared event of any kind, helps form the bonds that encourage closeness and comfort.

There's no hurry. We have a lifetime ahead of us to deepen our relationship. It will ripen naturally if we let it, accepting the newness and the discomfort as normal and temporary. Any good relationship takes time and effort. If we don't pressure ourselves, we may come to love each other genuinely.

I'm not sure anyone ever feels the same closeness to in-laws that we feel with our own original families. There's nothing wrong with that. There's a special bond between parents and their children that is seldom matched, although in some cases it does develop.

The fact that women tend to stay closer to their families helps those families feel less threatened by the new groom in their lives.

The man's family, on the other hand, frequently feels shut out when he abruptly disappears with his bride. They miss sharing his life. It doesn't occur to a lot of men to call Mom and say hello, while most women call home all the time. It would probably help everyone adjust more quickly if both the bride and groom kept up a caring intimacy with their own families, as well as with their in-laws.

> All we need to do is treat our in-laws like *friends,* rather than like family. With friends we're usually comfortable and easy and far less emotionally involved than we are with family.

The newlyweds can do a lot toward making each other's parents feel less threatened. Sending pictures to both sets of parents is just good sense. Continuing to show affection to their real parents is important, too, so no jealousy shows up there.

Young Jason might mention to his parents, "Joy's parents have been great to me; of course, they could never give me what you two have. You're the ones who helped me become who I am." (Not in front of Joy's parents, however, Jason.)

The best thing we can do for ourselves and each other is to expect that, naturally, our in-law will love his or her own family the most, and that gradually we'll all become closer anyway, by gentle exposure. All we need to do is treat our in-laws like *friends,* rather than like family. With friends we're usually comfortable and easy and far less emotionally involved than we are with family.

Maybe that's good. Perhaps it wouldn't hurt us a bit to treat our own children more like friends than like family. I would never go to a friend's home and say, "Donna, you should trim back your philodendrons; they're looking rangy." Alas, I confess I've said that very thing to Lisa.

Would I ever tell a friend, "Carolyn, don't you think you need a haircut?" Of course not. But I say it to Laurie without much hesitation. It's hard for us to keep our mouths shut because we get so used to telling our kids what we think they should do.

Maybe that little distance between parents- and kids-in-law is healthy. Certainly it's respectful to give them credit for being able to make their own decisions; respect we often don't give our own children. In dealing with in-laws, it's important to maintain a sense of respect, but with clear and honest communication.

Support Each Other

My friend Ann said the biggest problem in her marriage was the lack of support and understanding she got from her husband, especially when it came to her feelings about his parents. He acted as if all her complaints were just her imagination and refused to give them any importance at all.

That left her in a terribly uncomfortable position of aloneness, experiencing rejection from his family and being unable to find comfort from the most important person in her life. She found herself in a no-win position of disapproval from all sides; first her in-laws, then her husband if she looked to him for support. Of course she became more and more fearful.

The problem escalated when their daughter was born. Gertie, her mother-in-law, immediately stepped in and "took charge." She would constantly ignore Ann's wishes regarding the child's behavior. If Ann said, "Don't run in the house," Gertie would quickly tell the little girl, "It's okay to run in the house, dear." Ann felt more and more like a non-person, whose thoughts and words were meaningless. Eventually the marriage ended in divorce, and Ann looks back on the in-law situation as the chief cause.

She and I have talked about how she might have handled things differently if she'd been wiser in those days. "I never really confronted Gertie with what she was doing," Ann reflected. "I felt like *she* knew exactly what she was doing and chose to do it anyway, so talking about it wouldn't do any good. When I tried to tell my husband, he just cut me off as imagining things. If I were giving advice to someone in that same position, I'd say she should talk about it. A lot!"

I suspect a marriage counselor could have been helpful. Had Ann's self-esteem been a little better, she would have felt more justified in asserting herself, not letting herself be railroaded into submission. But she was too discouraged even to want to save the marriage after a few years of living with the noncommunicative, unsupportive husband, so she let the whole thing go.

An assertive wife might have said firmly to Gertie, "We have a problem. When you override my orders to Sally, I feel hurt because you act like I don't exist. Then I become angry because I feel you have no respect for me. I'm not willing to bring Sally to visit or even come myself unless we get this straightened out."

You can be sure Gertie would reconsider very quickly if it meant losing the company of the precious grandchild. And she should. She had the right to rear her own children however she chose, but Ann had that same right.

Take Care of Your Own Problems

I think Ann's husband was insensitive in not caring about her complaints, but I don't think he should have jumped in as the rescuer. We make a mistake in thinking the loved one in common should get everyone in harmony, because that's an impossible task for anyone. It's easy to see why we fall into that trap: We're afraid to make waves with the in-laws, so we prefer someone else doing it for us. Even if that person were willing and able to do it, however, we'd be stunting our own growth. It's good for us to settle our own disputes.

> We make a mistake in thinking the loved one in common should get everyone in harmony, because that's an impossible task for anyone.

I would have urged Ann's husband, however, to spend a lot of time listening to Ann, understanding her feelings and discussing her options with her. He might have said, "Honey, I feel bad that Mom makes you feel this way. I love you, and I don't want to see anyone hurt you. You know I'm behind you a hundred percent. You have my permission to tell anyone in my family how you feel about anything they do. I would want them to do the same with you. And I'll be happy to talk about your problems with you anytime you want."

That's the ideal, in my opinion, but few mates are that sensitive or skilled in relationship communication. If Ann's husband had been, they might still be married. Perhaps, then, their biggest problem was not in-laws, per se, but the lack of closeness between them because of his lack of sensitivity.

Letter to Your In-Law

Expecting your spouse to confront your in-law on your behalf only risks strain on your marriage. But how do you begin to assert yourself when you've been avoiding confrontation at all costs for this long? Try practicing first. Get your thoughts and feelings together by writing a letter *that you will never send, so be honest!* Get it all out, using as many specific details as possible. Put it away for a while.

When you come back to the letter, in an hour, a day, or a week, read it with one word in mind: fear. How does your fear affect the situations, thoughts, and feelings you describe in this letter? How does your in-law's fear come into play? Now take out another sheet of paper and write a response, as if you were your in-law.

When you've finished both letters, consider talking to your in-law or writing a letter that you *will* send. Perhaps you'd rather record a tape or send an e-mail. If you feel overwhelmed by the issues you have between you, focus instead on one recent situation and work your way gradually into others as you and your in-law become more comfortable discussing your relationship.

Too Many Cooks

There are many times when we're not sure where our responsibilities lie. If we're even halfway compassionate people, we hurt when we see someone we love hurting. Our tendency often is to jump in and help, whatever that may entail. But when we do that, we may only fan the fire and worsen an already uncomfortable situation.

Let's say a bride is put off by her father-in-law's manner. She complains to her husband, and she looks for sympathy as well from her own parents, brothers, and sisters. The groom feels terrible that his bride is uncomfortable, so he has a talk with his mother about what to do. Mom sympathizes, but she takes her husband's side and confides in their two daughters and son-in-law, all of whom resent the bride's selfishness. Bride, meanwhile, is getting pretty hostile with dad-in-law. She's going for more and more understanding to her own brothers, sister, and sister-in-law. Now, the sisters-in-law are strained in their relationship with the parents-in-law. The bride resents her brother-in-law's wife butting in and the groom's father is turning to the son's sister-in-law and her father. And if this doesn't make any sense to you, don't feel bad. I lost track somewhere in the first few sentences. But it shows the dynamics of "too many cooks" helping spoil a relationship; a common phenomenon that's almost the norm.

Everybody becomes a marriage counselor, giving advice to the bride and groom, and then they often become psychiatrists, analyzing the interaction of the entire extended family.

"Julie is paranoid. She thinks we spend all our time talking about her. Ha! I think that's called 'grandiosity.' Who does she think she is that we spend all our time thinking about her?"

"The one I'm worried about is John. I think he's neurotic. He never wants to do what the rest of us are doing. He's becoming a recluse."

"He says he just can't stand Melanie's attitude. He says she's manic-depressive, and he can't put up with her mood swings."

"She can't help that; she's an adult child of an alcoholic and grew up in a dysfunctional family. You notice how Melanie's always eating? That's because she's overly sensitive and can't assert herself. She needs to get help."

"What she needs is to divorce Mark. He is so totally irresponsible. All he has going for him are his looks. He's narcissistic."

> We have a responsibility to live our own lives as well as we can, and that takes plenty of energy. There's no need to try to live each other's as well—let them handle their own.

And so on. We all do it. Usually it's harmless, but it can get out of hand if people take themselves too seriously. They may begin to "choose up sides" and end up with gangs like the Jets and the Sharks, resulting in rumbles and wars at family dinners.

If you find yourself dreading the Fourth of July family picnic, know that you're not alone. Interacting with one's own family can often be difficult. And when you get a bunch of in-laws with *their* in-laws as well, you've got trouble.

The trick is to brainwash ourselves by saying over and over, "Live and let live." We have a responsibility to live our own lives as well as we can, and that takes plenty of energy. There's no need to try to live each other's as well—let them handle their own.

We can watch family dramas with interest, as we do soap operas or sit-coms, but we don't have to get involved emotionally any more than we would a TV show. We can be pleasant, respectful observers.

Worst-Case Scenarios

Sometimes, of course, there is just no hope of achieving a good relationship with in-laws. In rare situations you may marry into a family that is so swamped with pain and problems that they're absolutely miserable individuals. You may try to be nice, considerate, open, pleasing, thoughtful, and every other positive trait you can conjure up. Still you face nonacceptance and rejection.

You try to communicate respectfully. You pull out your best listening skills. You say "When you . . . I feel . . . because . . ."

sentences. You invite them over for dinner. You get only hostility in return.

Eventually you may decide to stop trying, because you're dealing with people who have been hurt so deeply and are carrying around such enormous loads of pain they're looking for someone to blame—and you're a handy target. At some point, in a case like that, retreat.

Retreating is not the same as rejecting. It isn't punishing with hostile coolness. It's simply giving the other party or parties the space they seem to want, not imposing your company on them, and yet, being as cordial as you would be toward any acquaintance.

Each of us gets to decide what we will do in any circumstance. For instance, Ann might have said to her mother-in-law, "Gertie, I'll be happy to come to Thanksgiving dinner, but if you overrule my instructions to Sally, we'll leave."

Then Ann will leave when she's undermined, pleasantly but promptly. "Bye, everybody, see you soon. Dinner was great, Gertie. C'mon, Sally." Her husband may stay or leave, that's his choice. Ann is taking care of her needs.

We wouldn't be happy doing that kind of thing if it were selfish or unfair—only after we've given the matter plenty of thought and have come to terms with what is fair and respectful to both parties. But this is a last resort. Usually we don't have to go that far to get along with our in-laws. Most of them are just like us, wanting a good relationship and wondering how to achieve it.

Letting go of expectations can really help. My young neighbor was bemoaning the fact that she'd always wanted a "fun" mother-in-law, and hers was not the least bit fun.

"She deprived me of that dream," Nancy said, a bit resentfully. "I wanted us to be cool

> Eventually you may decide to stop trying, because you're dealing with people who have been hurt so deeply and are carrying around such enormous loads of pain they're looking for someone to blame—and you're a handy target.

together, to do a lot of things like going shopping and having lunch out, but she's not interested. Life's a serious business to her."

That's too bad, and I wish Nancy could have a fun mom-in-law. All she can really do is make sure she has fun friends and try to be as lighthearted with her mother-in-law as she comfortably can. If she changes her expectations to "I want a polite, cordial relationship with my in-laws," she'll feel less cheated.

Steps for a Better Relationship with Your In-Laws

Here's my best advice for being (and dealing with) an in-law:

1. Lower expectations of yourself. Don't beat yourself up if you're not immediately enthralled with your in-laws. Quit feeling like you "should" love them. (As Albert Ellis says, "Don't should on yourself.") And give them the same permission not to be crazy about you.

2. Accept the fact that you're different from one another. You each have a lifetime of different experiences, different ancestry, different belief systems, different likes and dislikes, and different goals. Perhaps the only thing you have in common is the person you love. Don't feel guilty that you're not alike. It's good for families to get "new blood," and our ways tend to rub off on each other. Look at the differences as fresh viewpoints, but not as barriers you have to overcome or change. You both have the right to stay exactly the way you are if you so choose.

3. Recognize the problem between you as fear. It's much less threatening when you can see through the apparent

hostility and find the scared child underneath. Know that no matter how old the cold, defensive person may be, he or she is still a scared child when it comes to in-law relationships.

4. Don't be dishonest, but temper honesty with kindness. An honest relationship doesn't mean brutal frankness, which can be hurtful—it does mean plenty of conversation and describing of feelings.

5. Mutual respect must always be present. Not only do you need to respect your in-laws, but you absolutely must respect yourself as well. If you always consider their wishes and feelings while ignoring your own, you're going to build up enormous resentment that will inevitably be destructive. Admittedly, it's tough to decide where the balance is as you try to respect both parties, but it's essential to respect both yourself and your in-laws.

6. Consider all the in-laws as friends. Friendships develop quickly or slowly, deeply or shallowly, but any of them can enhance our lives if we allow them to go at their own pace.

7. Don't look to your mate to solve your problems for you. Nor should you feel responsible for being the go-between for your spouse and your family. Do, however, make sure all the people concerned know they have your permission to discuss their concerns with the appropriate parties. Be attentive and interested, and lovingly encourage them to do something about their problems. You don't have to take sides. Certainly, if someone's actions are affecting your life, you, too, have the right to talk to that person about it. But the kindest thing you can do is to involve yourself in your mate's feelings and leave the actual solving to him or her.

—14—

Little Things
Mean a Lot

When you were a little kid, who washed the windows in your house, Mom or Dad? Who put gas in the car? Who did the laundry, the yard work, the painting? Did Dad get up on Sunday morning and make pancakes? Was it Mom's job to trim the Christmas tree?

Whatever you observed in those early days helped you form your expectations of who does what job in marriage. You learn those "truths" without realizing they're not chiseled in stone. Then you proceed into your own marriage, fully expecting the other person to share those same beliefs.

None of us wants to do things we find especially unpleasant, but most of us have decided which responsibilities we're willing to consider taking on.

"I will never clean toilets," Victoria told me firmly. "Daddy did that; it's not women's work."

There's nothing wrong with Victoria's belief about the required sex of toilet cleaners, unless she marries Jake who says firmly, "I'm not about to clean the toilet. I wouldn't even know how; Mother never taught me. A man shouldn't have to clean a toilet."

He, too, has every right to his conviction, but what do they do now? Both firmly believe they're right, and they're not about to consider changing their stances.

Cooperation Techniques

So what else is new? Their problem is par for the course and certainly one that's solvable. It requires only mutual respect and the desire to cooperate. (Actually that's true of every aspect of marriage. Perhaps I needn't have written this book at all, but just stated, "A happy marriage requires only mutual respect and the desire to cooperate!") But maybe I can share some suggestions I've picked up from other couples who have found good ways to promote cooperation.

Chore Cards

One method comes from an Episcopalian priest who said, "My wife and I made up a card game. We write down on three-by-five cards all the chores that need to be done. We sit down and take cards we're willing to be responsible for, but both of us understand it's not a permanent assignment. Any time one of us wants to change jobs, we ask for a new game and start to negotiate.

"For instance, last week I told Mary Anne that I was tired of taking out the trash, and I wanted to trade that card for one of hers. She was sick of being responsible for getting babysitters, and we agreed that was a fair trade. I took the babysitter card and she took the trash one. We'll live by that until one of us requests another card game, and then we'll trade around again."

"You make it sound wonderfully simple," I said. "Is it always such an easy exchange? What if Mary Anne does not want to take out the trash?"

"Sometimes it takes a lot of finagling," he admitted. "Sometimes we sit there for hours trying to agree on what's fair; but we always do eventually, maybe out of sheer exhaustion. We've gotten good at negotiating. One of us might say, 'I'll trade cleaning up the dog poop for paying the bills.' The other might say, 'No way.

I enjoy writing checks, but I loathe cleaning up dog poop.' Maybe it might take two jobs to replace one, like, 'I'll pay the bills and keep the cars gassed up if you'll agree to pick up after Poochie.' "

Any arrangement is fine, as long as both people agree on it. The division of labor shouldn't ever be permanently defined, in my opinion, unless *both* people happen to love their job responsibilities and have no desire to change. I liked George and Mary Anne's creative solution as much as they did.

> The division of labor shouldn't ever be permanently defined, in my opinion, unless *both* people happen to love their job responsibilities and have no desire to change.

The only time it wouldn't be successful, it seems, is if one or both parties lost the desire to cooperate and made the whole thing a power struggle. I could see either spouse refusing to give up a card or setting the exchange so high the other couldn't comply. Because power struggles never solve a problem, when one occurs, it must be recognized and dealt with for cooperation to resume.

"I'm discouraged. We've been sitting here for two hours and nothing I suggest will let me get rid of the window-washing job. You seem determined not to take that over no matter how much I offer to do in exchange. And I'm sick of washing windows. What do you suggest?" Asking for suggestions often creates an atmosphere of respect that begins to inspire actual problem solving. Instead of tenaciously refusing to cooperate, the uncooperative partner may begin to think of new solutions.

"Maybe we should hire a window-washing service." Or, "Could we pay the kid across the street to do it?" Or even, "Windows just get dirty again; why wash them at all?"

Redefining "Fair"

For the most part we seem more willing to do the jobs that fit with our picture of how life should be. Having a clean house is more my priority than Larry's, so I'm more willing to make it happen. But I'm

> The whole issue of responsibilities is a constantly changing picture as each of us moves into different ages and roles.

certainly not going to be responsible for all of it, nor would he expect me to be.

It doesn't seem fair that one person take more responsibility for household chores than the other. Nor is it necessarily fair that one be more responsible for earning money than the other. It all boils down to a division of labor in which both parties are equally responsible for the good of the family unit.

Traditionally men hunted the animals and women cooked them. Some of us still like our roles defined exactly that way. Many men are the breadwinners and women the homemakers. That's perfect when both like that arrangement.

But more and more women find a lot of pleasure in working outside the home, as men do, and are contributing sizeable incomes to the running of the home. Men have changed their priorities to allow for more time with the children, and I heartily applaud that attitude.

The best arrangement, as far as I'm concerned, would be letting both Mom and Dad work at an outside job half the time and take care of the house and children the other half. It's good for us to experience what our mates have to do—or get to do. (Probably most of us suspect the other person has it easier than we do.) But few of us could get half-time jobs that would make that arrangement feasible, so we have to work within the system we have.

The whole issue of responsibilities is a constantly changing picture as each of us moves into different ages and roles. So, like George and Mary Anne, we need to expect changes and allow for them.

If we look at each phase as simply a different job description rather than a sentence to hard labor, we can handle it easily. What makes the issue difficult is our belief system that is filled with shoulds and oughts and expectations that have practically become moral values.

Wouldn't it be great if we could wipe the slate clean and start our marital working arrangement from scratch?

I remember my mother looking at all the bright new towels we got as wedding presents and saying, "How nice that you get to start out with towels that all match!" She had a collection of colors and styles that had accumulated over the years and were still "too good to throw out," so the bathroom displayed a strange and sometimes jarring assortment.

We could look at our expectations and beliefs the same way. We have so many that are old and shabby, but we hang onto them without realizing they could be replaced with new beliefs, and it wouldn't even cost the price of new towels! It would cost only our time in conversation.

We'd have to be willing to discard all the shoulds. Our purpose would be to think of all the ways either of us might contribute to the family unit and simply divide them up according to our skills, as well as our preferences.

My daughter Laurie, who edits all my books for me, is a bright, creative woman who loves her job at an advertising agency. She's never been a homemaker. Turning out a gourmet dinner or polishing the furniture does not fill her heart with joy like creating sparkling copy or producing a successful TV commercial.

Her husband, Pete, on the other hand, doesn't find pleasure in a job. Unlike many men whose egos are directly connected to work, Pete is happy running marathons and competing in Scrabble tournaments and "pondering." When their son Christopher was born, they worked out a great arrangement in which Pete was the primary caretaker of the baby and house while Laurie brought home paychecks. She took part in Christopher's care, to be sure, but Pete was largely responsible. It worked well for all three of them.

Any arrangement is workable. The hardest part is getting rid of old, stereotyped beliefs.

Decisions Based on Who You Are, Not Who You "Should" Be

Our preferences as well as our skills should help determine our delegated chores. Generally, we think of women as the official seamstresses. (I don't even think there's a word for male "seamsters.") One of my female clients has finally put her foot down and announced to her family that they may use the sewing machine anytime they want, but she's given up sewing forever.

Her husband happens to be a detail-oriented, patient man, good with his hands. He sews on scout badges with invisible stitches.

She's good at painting entire rooms quickly, while he painstakingly does the careful trimming. It finally made sense to them that he is better suited to sewing and mending and she is better suited to mowing the lawn with the power mower.

It makes me wonder how many roles we're stuck in simply by tradition. It might open wonderful new areas of interest when we begin to investigate what we're doing because we want to, and what we're doing because of society's expectations.

Time Tracking

Many times my clients are angry at what they see as an unfair division of labor.

Margo said, "I work an eight-hour day at a print shop. Then I come home and clean the house, cook the dinner, take care of the kids' needs, do the laundry, clean up the dishes, make everyone's lunches for the next day, get the kids bathed and in bed, then fall into bed myself, exhausted. James puts in his time at the office and that's it."

Unfair, right? But listen to James.

"Hey, I'm not a jerk. First of all I work a good ten to twelve hours every day. I have to work that much overtime to pay for the huge new house Margo had to have. I pay for a cleaning lady twice a week. A lot of the time we all eat out; it's not like she cooks many meals. And also I'm willing to do my share of the housework—it's just that I don't do it 'right,' which is how Margo thinks it 'should' be done. She thinks none of us does anything right, so she has to do it herself. No wonder she's exhausted. She never rests; but it's sure not my fault, the way she makes it sound."

In this case, the problem was Margo's need to be Wonder Woman. Sometimes, though, a husband or wife is not putting in an equal share. One of the techniques I suggest as a kind of measuring stick is this:

Put a large piece of paper or poster board on the kitchen counter or any handy place where you can both jot down time spent on anything you do for the good of the family unit. For a week or two, keep track of your times. Then you'll see in black and white how equally your labor is divided. It's a bit of a nuisance, writing it all down, but it also becomes kind of fun as you watch your efforts get recorded. In fact, sometimes people begin working extra hard so they can prove they're doing the lion's share.

If you work an eight-hour shift someplace, you get to record not only the eight hours, but also your travel time to and from work. Jot down seventeen minutes stopping at the grocery store, thirty-eight minutes preparing dinner, forty-two minutes bathing kids and reading them their stories, and so on.

On the weekend you get credit for yard work, washing cars, driving kids to soccer practice, anything at all that contributes to the good of the family. Watching TV doesn't count. Somebody asked, "What about reading the paper? It should count. I'm keeping abreast of what's going on in the world, and then I'm better able to keep the children informed."

I think that's reaching. If we went that far, we could excuse almost any activity as beneficial to the family. "Getting my hair done makes me feel so much better, I'm a nicer wife and mother the whole rest of the day, so I should be allowed to count hairdresser time." I don't think so.

"What about helping the neighbor with his cooler? That's not leisure time. Can't I count that?" No. It's wonderful to help your neighbor, but it doesn't affect your family's well-being. Fixing your own cooler certainly counts.

It takes a little time figuring out what you can and can't count, but usually you come to agree on the guidelines. Sometimes it becomes clear that one person really is badly overloaded. Other times both people see that their work is pretty evenly divided. I think it's well worth the small amount of time it takes if you find yourselves arguing about pulling your weight. At least you can both see the fairness or unfairness you've been arguing about.

How Money Affects Responsibility

There are no right or wrong ways to divvy up the labor, only workable plans that suit both people. Like any partnership, marriage is full of shared responsibilities, including the responsibility of money.

Generally speaking, money is power. The person who earns it often has the most power in the relationship. The other person often feels like a second-class citizen, whether or not he or she should.

It's demeaning for anyone to have to ask for money, and yet many non-working spouses get none unless they do. One of my neighbors must ask for the exact amount of money she will need to buy the groceries or give the kids for lunch money. Her husband insists on an accurate accounting of all she spends. Needless to say, she no longer loves him at all. She's staying only until the children are old enough to be on their own. Then she'll be out of there—unless they make some changes.

> Generally speaking, money is power. The person who earns it often has the most power in the relationship.

Other marriages work on an allowance basis. Both partners get a certain amount of money they can spend as they please. The amount is exactly the same for both. That's a pretty fair arrangement if both are working equally for the good of the family.

When Laurie and Pete got married, they formed a corporation called Acme Dynamics Ltd. It existed only in their minds, but it's the "business" that provides the operating expenses for their marriage. They were both earning money and they decided that each of them would put a certain percentage of their income into Acme Dynamics to pay for rent, utilities, food, insurance and other necessities. When Pete quit his job to take care of Christopher, Laurie put her entire income into Acme, which paid them both an equal allowance every month.

It isn't a bad idea to have a "business" within the marriage. Marriage is made up of so many facets, and the businesslike part of it is one we seldom consider beforehand. We never dream that money will be a problem when we're in love.

> But we don't have to have the same values. We just have to respect each other's right to have different ones.

In fact, money is a big problem in many marriages. It needn't be if it's discussed and decisions are made jointly in a respectful way. It gets out of proportion when people carry around resentment over unresolved money issues.

Larry and I started out earning nearly equal salaries, but when we had babies, we agreed I would quit my job. Even though I was eager to stay home and be a mother, wife, and homemaker, I really missed having money I felt was mine, to do whatever I wanted with.

Larry didn't feel like the "powerful one," but I felt he was because our sustenance depended solely on him. Very soon I started teaching piano at home so I could have something to spend as I pleased. That's how we got into the habit we're still into today: His money buys most of our necessities; mine buys non-necessities. We're both comfortable with that. I will happily furnish the entire house with my income, but I'd die before I'd buy a loaf of bread. The arrangement works because we both think it's fine.

We have a difference of opinion on what to do with extra money. He likes to spend his on experiences and I like to spend mine on things.

Actually, it works out well because I get to go on vacations he pays for, and he gets to live in the snazzy new room I fixed up. From time to time we shake our heads in mild disapproval at the other's ways, but we no longer feel strong disapproval at each other's peculiarities. He just can't see why I would buy new carpeting when the old is "still good," and I can't imagine his spending that much money for a river raft trip down the Grand Canyon.

But we don't have to have the same values. We just have to respect each other's right to have different ones.

These differences are minor, I realize, compared to people who see their spouses "throwing away money" on alcohol or hobbies, or anything else that takes away from the necessities of life. And this seems to happen fairly often. One party will be a spendthrift while the other has to scrimp to pay for groceries.

That's unfair, of course, and needs to be dealt with if there's going to be any harmony in the relationship. Sometimes it helps to consult a marriage or financial counselor, a pastor or rabbi, or any respected advisor.

Some folks swear by budgets. Some use the envelope system, where you put so much money in envelopes for rent, clothes, movies, and so forth. Some prefer to spend it as they get it and suffer the consequences when they run out.

The point I'm making is that almost *nobody* finds finances to be problem-free, except maybe the very wealthy. But that's okay. It just means you have to talk and talk and talk as you work out compromises. And sometimes you have to shut up, too. One wife confided that she had argued with her husband for months about some scuba gear he wanted to buy. When she finally backed off and said, "I guess if you can find the money for it, you should go ahead and get it," he said, "I guess I can't really afford it," and that was the end of that.

Which proves that money can often turn into the basis of a power struggle, just like anything else can. Sometimes the actual dollars have less to do with our arguments than does the desire to "win."

It's good to remind ourselves that the family unit is a cooperative venture in which everyone involved pulls his own weight as much as he's able. The man and woman expend energy on a relatively equal basis to take care of their own and the other's needs. As the children grow they lend their energies to caring for *their* own and others' needs. No one except babies, young children, and pets should get a free ride in life.

It doesn't matter whether we contribute by baking pies or earning corporate-president salaries, as long as we contribute fairly. Neither partner should feel superior by virtue of his financial capacity; nor should he feel inferior, as long as he's being as productive a member as he's able.

But why is money such a sticky subject in marriage? I think it's symbolic of character in our minds. We don't want to be thought of as "tight," "spendthrift," or "selfish," so we may hesitate to speak up about our feelings. Even if we do express ourselves, we may go along with our partners' wishes rather than risk disapproval. But then we build up resentments that do more harm than if we'd stood our ground in the first place.

> It doesn't matter whether we contribute by baking pies or earning corporate-president salaries, as long as we contribute fairly.

I'm thinking of a woman I worked with who had brought a "nice nest egg" of family stocks and bonds into her marriage and had watched it all disappear in a two-year period as her husband invested in high-risk ventures. She had believed in his business expertise at first, but when she became alarmed at how much they'd lost, she still allowed him to use the stocks because she felt "a wife should." Finally, they were reduced to selling their house and renting a small apartment. She was relegated to making hamburgers in a fast-food place, bitter at what her lifestyle had become.

Was it her moral obligation as a wife to make those funds available to her husband for investment? That would be a dandy conversation piece for your next dinner party, because you'd get a lot of strong and varied reactions. Some people would say, "Of course it was. Marriage means both people contribute all they own for the common good."

Some would argue, "It wasn't good sense to lose everything when obviously the man was lacking fiscal skills."

And some might answer, "If she expected to share in the rewards if his investments paid off, she should be willing to share the unsuccessful outcome as well."

It beats me. I tend to believe, however, that both parties should be entitled to keep savings or funds that were family heritages unless, of course, they're needed for food and shelter. Speculation should be done only if one can afford it, and it seems to me the little nest egg should have been held in safety. If I had been that wife, I think I would have said a kind, firm "no" when my husband asked for the stocks. But as a starry-eyed bride, I probably would have done exactly what she did: given a reluctant "Yes" because I loved my knight in shining armor so much I wouldn't have been expecting problems up ahead. So *love* clouds the issue of financial negotiation within marriage, making it difficult to work out wise decisions because they're emotionally colored.

I know a husband whose wife went through thousands of dollars (his) buying expensive gifts for her family. She explained, "When I love someone, I like to show it by buying nice things for them; it's not like we can't afford it."

He was feeling guilty about his resentment, unsure of whether he should set some kind of limit, afraid he'd be called a *cheapskate*. And he was scared of the eventual outcome if she continued buying at the rate she'd been buying so far.

Often one person tends to be practical and frugal; the other an easy spender. Neither is necessarily right or wrong, but it's tough when they're stuck with solving their differences.

The only answer I see is continued respectful communication to seek answers that both will feel OK about. Admittedly, it's not easy. We need to keep shoulds and oughts out of it, and not allow tears or anger to interfere. Always remember to stop the conversation when it gets too emotional, but be sure to come back to it when feelings are again under control (see chapter 7).

No solution has to be the final statement. It's good to say, "All right, let's try this way for a [month, quarter, year, whatever] and see how it works. If we don't like it we can always try another way."

I really believe that most of us are good people, not out to cheat our partners. Our difficulties come mostly as we wrestle with what's fair and unfair in dealing with those we love. We can be most effective in finding compromises if we stay gentle and always honest.

Who's Responsible?

The following statements are open-ended to allow you both to discuss your expectations and definitions of what a husband or wife should be solely responsible for and what they should share the responsibility for. Make a copy of this exercise or use pens of different colors. After each statement, circle "husband" if you think the husband should be responsible; "wife" if you think the wife should be responsible; "both" if they should equally share responsibility; "neither" if you don't think the statement applies to either of you.

If you and your partner agree that husbands and wives are, in theory, equally responsible for everything (and therefore would circle "both" for all statements), then use this exercise for your roles specifically. For example, if the wife is a seasoned gardener, you might circle "wife" after "Should take care of the yard work"—not because you see this as the role of all wives but because you see it as a logical use of skills in your particular household. Even on this, you may not agree!

Circle One

1. Should have the final say in decision making:

    wife   husband   both   neither

2. Should have total financial responsibility:

    wife   husband   both   neither

3. Should take care of the house repairs:

    wife   husband   both   neither

4. Should take care of the yard work:

    wife   husband   both   neither

5. Should discipline the children:

    wife   husband   both   neither

continues

6. Has a right to sexual relationships upon request:
   wife   husband both   neither

7. Should never do *any* housework:
   wife   husband both   neither

8. Should take care of the following types of housework:

dusting	wife	husband	both	neither
vacuuming	wife	husband	both	neither
toilets	wife	husband	both	neither
floors	wife	husband	both	neither
windows	wife	husband	both	neither
trash	wife	husband	both	neither
dishes	wife	husband	both	neither
laundry	wife	husband	both	neither

9. Should be allowed to go out alone once a week:
   wife   husband   both   neither

10. Should call home when he/she is going to be late:
    wife   husband   both   neither

11. Should do things with the family:
    wife   husband   both   neither

12. Should control the TV programs when home:
    wife   husband   both   neither

13. Should change a baby's diaper:
    wife   husband   both   neither

14. Is entitled to as much free time as she/he wants:
    wife   husband   both   neither

15. Should think of parents before spouse:
    wife   husband   both   neither

16. Should show affection at all times:
    wife   husband   both   neither

17. Should never cry:
    wife   husband   both   neither

18   Should be allowed friendships with the opposite sex:
wife   husband   both   neither

19. Should host parties for family, friends and/or coworkers:
wife   husband   both   neither

20. Should share a hobby or interest with spouse:
wife   husband   both   neither

21. Should have some privacy on occasion:
wife   husband   both   neither

22. Should be involved in the religious life of the family:
wife   husband   both   neither

23. Should be the only one to initiate love-making:
wife   husband   both   neither

24. Should cook:
wife   husband   both   neither

25. Should plan the social life of the family:
wife   husband   both   neither

26. Should have a career:
wife   husband   both   neither

27. Should do all the shopping for the family:
wife   husband   both   neither

28. Should never refuse sex with spouse:
wife   husband   both   neither

29. Should never talk back to spouse:
wife   husband   both   neither

30. Should handle all car maintenance:
wife   husband   both   neither

31. Should handle all pet care:
wife   husband   both   neither

32. Should remember birthdays, anniversaries, etc., of friends and family:
wife   husband   both   neither

═══ 15 ═══

The Way We Were

The bride and groom heard the question and they easily concurred, "I do." They meant it. Death! Lifetime! Commitment! Yeah!

But somewhere along the way they began to have misgivings and say, "I didn't know it was going to be like *this!*" They watched their friends get divorced and it might have seemed appealing. These are some of the things couples tell me:

"As I look back, I don't think I was ever really in love with her. We dated, we liked each other. All our friends were getting married and we just kind of got swept away, too. It was the thing to do at the time."

"I was miserable living with my parents. He was a perfect way out."

"We had this great physical attraction, but after the honeymoon she lost interest in sex. I can't be expected to live in a sexless marriage, can I?"

"His mother dominates every thought he has. He's really married to *her.*"

"She just wants to party all the time. I want a wife who will have kids and cook. We ought to work together on our house, but she's never home."

"I thought I knew him, but I didn't. I still don't. He doesn't talk."

"Hey, I can tolerate anything but infidelity. I can't get the picture out of my mind of her with that other guy."

"If he'd quit drinking, maybe we could make it work, but he won't."

"I've always come second to the kids."

"I've always come second to his job."

How much do we have to suffer before we're allowed to divorce? Are we *ever* justified? What if one wants out and the other doesn't?

There are so many options in life. Each choice we make has a price tag. Marriage is one of the best institutions around, but it has one of the highest costs. It is enormously expensive in terms of the energy necessary to keep it healthy.

Marriage Types

There are at least two kinds of marriages that can work splendidly:

First is the old-fashioned arrangement that many conservative Christians still believe is the best way. The husband is the head of the house, and he loves his wife as much as he loves himself. He takes care of her as well as he does his own body. He loves her as Christ loves the church. She is submissive to him, allows him to make the major decisions in their life, and she looks to him for guidance. Together they make a great combination. It works!

> Marriage is one of the best institutions around, but it has one of the highest costs.

Second is the more modern arrangement that appeals to many couples today: the marriage of equal partners. Neither person is the "boss" or decision-maker, but both make decisions equally. Neither is responsible for the other's well-being, but both love the other so much they nurture each other by choice. There is cooperation between them and respect for each other's rights. Together they make a great combination. It works!

I know people from both styles, and I believe both have the potential for success.

Conservative Marriage

The marriages based on conservative Christian teaching are extremely happy if they're composed of special people who make God the center of their life together. The level of love required to insure the success of these marriages is exemplary, but because many people just can't seem to sustain it, we don't see good ones all around us.

A friend who has one of these marriages says, "There's no woman on earth who wouldn't follow a man who leads lovingly and gently."

By and large I agree with her. But it isn't easy for men to measure up to society's standards and still be the loving, gentle leaders their wives are looking for. They get caught up in building their careers, as a rule, and their primary focus becomes their jobs. Once wives feel like they're "playing second fiddle" to their husbands' work, they lose some of their willingness to "obey, praise, and honor."

And hell hath no fury as a woman scorned. When women feel less important than their men's other interests, we can get downright nasty! Then there's a vicious circle. Both people want that loving closeness, but when they feel it lessening, they respond out of fear and often behave badly. They use anger or pouting, crying or withdrawing, drinking or overeating, and many manipulative efforts to "get" the other person to love them again.

The more you distance yourself from me, the more I will distance myself from you, until we have a chicken-and-egg routine that often worsens as we blame each other for causing it.

"If he loved me, I'd be the kind, nurturing, sexy wife he wants."

"If she acted lovingly, I'd be there showing how much I love her."

Women want men to be those loving, gentle romantics we dream about. Yet, in truth, some men who have those qualities may seem too passive for us. If they're sensitive and communicative, and good at sharing feelings, they might not be the strong, aggressive men women admire as "successful." It's almost impossible for a man to be a combination of all those traits.

Men want women who are loving, gentle, and romantic as well, but they often become annoyed if we're too dependent on them. They want us to be responsible for ourselves and not lean on them for everything. In fact, they often admire strong, assertive women even though they may be threatened by them at the same time. Women can't possibly be the perfect combination, either.

Marriages that last, then, will be between people who are wise enough to accept imperfection; those who can live and let live for the most part and not let their happiness be determined by their mate's behavior.

Marriage Based on Equality

That takes us to the other type of marriage I know can be successful: the equality arrangement in which neither person is submissive to or responsible for the other one. But that's just as hard to carry off as the first kind we looked at.

In the relationship of equality, neither person has the right to expect to be "taken care of " by the other. Ideally, we'll love each other enough to want to be loving and caring and willing to share each other's burdens and joys. But if I'm unhappy, it's my fault.

Independent partners develop a lot of strength and gain continuing confidence as they strive to fill their own needs while also being helpmates to their spouses.

Sometimes, though, they lose a lot of the closeness they could have in a more interdependent relationship. Both people might become so fiercely independent that they're "married singles." They share the house, children, and occasional meals, but find most of their pleasure separately. The common bond weakens as they find themselves only good friends. There's still a lot of caring and respect between them, but it's not as strong a marriage as it could be.

When Marriages Are in Trouble

No wonder we find ourselves discouraged when all the avenues are so fraught with difficulties. A successful marriage takes two people who are really dedicated to having a good marriage.

Yesterday I saw a couple in my office who were already having doubts about their commitment, though they'd been married just two years. (Many people don't make it past a year!)

"I think maybe it was a mistake we married in the first place," said Gary. "I feel like I've lost all my freedom. I'm twenty-one, Leslie's twenty, but our lives aren't fun anymore. I still want to go out and party and she just wants to stay home. She doesn't want me to go alone. If I do, she gets so upset I don't even enjoy myself."

Both people might become so fiercely independent that they're "married singles." They share the house, children, and occasional meals, but find most of their pleasure separately.

Leslie added, "I can't trust him. He's already had an affair with another woman. He's cute, everyone loves him. But after a few drinks, he loses his head. I'm very religious; don't drink; don't like to party. I want to have a baby, but he doesn't want the responsibility. He wants to run around like a young kid. I feel so sad, like the wonderful bond between us has been broken. I'm not sure I can ever love him like I used to."

My heart went out to both of them. They are young. I can't help wondering if they didn't marry in haste and youthful excitement, and maybe it was a poor decision. But now what do they do?

Before You Give Up

I always admit to clients that I have a bias toward helping people stay married if it can be worked out. Even if just *one* person wants it,

> On the other hand, staying together "for the sake of the children" isn't always the best thing, either. Children don't gain much stability in a home filled with anger and resentment.

I try very hard to see if the problems can be resolved so they'll both choose to continue the marriage. But if one or both clearly doesn't want to work at it, I know I'm licked. Still, I try to find out how I can help them.

One of the questions I ask is whether they have spiritual convictions that marriage is forever. Some people say, "Yeah, I believe it's supposed to be permanent, but I know I can't live this way anymore. Next time I'll make a better choice. That one will be forever."

Some say they have no religious belief about marriage. They see it as strictly societal.

Sometimes one believes one way and one the other. Thank goodness it isn't my place to judge their beliefs. Most of the time I'm able to view the situation objectively and help them arrive at whatever resolution seems the best to them. But it's a lot harder when there are children who will be hurt if the marriage dissolves. On the other hand, staying together "for the sake of the children" isn't always the best thing, either. Children don't gain much stability in a home filled with anger and resentment.

The whole question of commitment confuses me. I confess that to my clients. I'm willing to help them untangle feelings and problems. I will be the calm, objective "outsider" who looks for untried solutions and attempts to keep the atmosphere respectful and productive. But I'm glad I'm not the one who has to decide whether the marriage should continue—that's their responsibility.

There seem to be three possible states of married life. The worst is full of unhappiness, anger, hurt, lack of communication and closeness. It's the most likely to end in divorce.

In the middle group, the partners have sunk into a kind of apathy, resigning themselves to a mediocre, ordinary, lackluster relationship. It might last for years, but neither person will enjoy it much.

The best, of course, is that of bliss. A supreme kind of joy that shows in both people's faces when they see each other or even talk about each other. It's the state most of us think we're getting when we marry, but it's the most elusive. Many of us get to experience it only for a year or two in the beginning.

Is it ever too late to achieve that state? I don't think so. No matter how many times we've been hurt by each other, we always have the capacity to try again.

Stockbrokers get shrewder at handling investments as they work at the skill year after year. Photographers become adept at choosing shutter speeds as they take more and more pictures. Gardeners become both scientists and artists through their years of dealing with aphids and fertilizers. Chefs produce better epicurean dishes, beauticians create better haircuts, and musicians perform ever more beautifully.

We can get better at anything if we practice it. So in spite of thousands of disappointments and setbacks in our marriage, we always have the ability to improve our skills in relating to each other.

> No matter how many times we've been hurt by each other, we always have the capacity to try again.

Counseling

One good way to start (or continue) is marriage counseling. For many of us that seems like a scary thing to do. We hate to admit we could use help in dealing with what "should" be something we can handle ourselves.

I remember the first time Larry and I agreed we might benefit from counseling. I made the appointment, then canceled it. I made it again, and canceled it again. Each time we were a couple of days away from the meeting, we talked each other out of going. "It'll be all right; we can solve this alone," we told ourselves.

That's pretty common behavior. If the first appointment is a hard hurdle for you, you'll feel nervous but should go anyway. You'll probably find you actually enjoy having someone helping you.

If you haven't a clue which counselor to call and you have the courage to share with a friend that you're considering counseling, you'll find recommendations coming out of the woodwork. *Everybody's* been to counseling, it seems. When someone glows as he talks about the counselor who helped him and his wife, take him seriously. He wouldn't be recommending someone who left him lukewarm.

You have a right to know what kind of credibility a counselor has. What level of education? In some states, anyone can be a counselor just by hanging out a sign. Look for someone trained at no less than a Master's level, or with training from a religious facility you know and trust.

Look them up in the *Yellow Pages* (usually under "Marriage Counselors") and ask about fees. Don't be embarrassed. It's a perfectly acceptable question, especially in this relationship where honesty is valued. You can almost always find a counselor who's willing to work with you if you have trouble paying all at once, and many have sliding scales. Your medical insurance plan might pay for at least a portion of counseling.

Feel free to ask about affiliations. It's reassuring to know your therapist belongs to some associations that demand certain standards be met by their members. One major one is the American Association for Marriage and Family Therapy. The National Academy of Certified Clinical Mental Health Counselors is another reputable one, as are the National Board for Certified Counselors and the American Association for Counseling and Development.

There are a few psychiatrists who do marriage counseling, but most of them refer patients to counselors. Look for letters: Ph.D., M.Ed., Ed.D., M.A., or M.S.W., all indicating graduate degrees.

When you choose a counselor, give yourself permission to try one session. It's important to find someone with whom you feel comfortable. If you don't, by all means don't go back. There are so many styles of counselors, you can find one with whom you'll relate well. You might need to shop around and try two or three in order to settle on the one who seems helpful and insightful, as well as comfortable. Look for someone who obviously understands you.

It's important to be honest. The counseling process will be much less lengthy and costly if everything said is truthful. A therapist may be fooled by a client's lies, but the problems can't possibly be solved, so it's a waste of time and money not to be honest.

You might be slightly nervous at first, but that will disappear as you begin feeling at home. Anything people do for the first time often causes a little anxiety in the beginning.

Thank goodness the days are almost gone when there was a stigma attached to counseling. People used to think of it as something only crazy people needed. Now, it's not only acceptable, there's a certain amount of pride evident in many people who talk openly about their therapy.

I look at it much like taking a class. We're learning new information in a comfortable "classroom" where the teacher is focusing all his or her energy on only us. It's wonderful! We can ask all the questions we want, and they'll always be answered with respect and understanding. It's private; no one laughs or makes fun of us, and we feel more acceptance there than almost anywhere else. Not only that, all three of us are there with a common objective: To make this couple happier! Can you beat that for a great way to spend an hour?

One important bit of advice: Do what the counselor suggests, as far as homework. Sometimes couples come back week after week admitting a little sheepishly that they didn't have time to talk to each other. You don't want to waste your money on advice designed to help you if you're going to disregard it.

Larry and I have had marriage counseling with five different counselors in our forty-nine years together. We've benefited more from some than others, but both of us agree each one has given us something positive with which to work. We still quote lines from all five counselors. And they'd probably be pleased to know how much they live on in our lives.

Being both a counselor and a counselee, I know how it feels to risk. People often look embarrassed and ask, "This will be confidential, won't it?"

I can't emphasize enough that any reputable counselor is aware of the need for confidentiality. For counselors to slip and reveal anything would be risking their entire reputation and, therefore, their livelihood. They don't dare. Feel perfectly confident that your secrets won't leave the room.

The funny thing is, your secrets are way more common than you may think. There isn't any new behavior in this world. The things you're saying have been said before, probably many times over. Human beings make the same mistakes and have the same feelings, thoughts, and doubts that human beings have always had and will continue having. Your counselor won't be shocked.

> Human beings make the same mistakes and have the same feelings, thoughts, and doubts that human beings have always had and will continue having. Your counselor won't be shocked.

What if you want to get counseling and your partner refuses? Go anyway. While it is much quicker and easier to help a marriage improve if both parties participate in counseling, a lot can be accomplished with only one. As you learn what you're doing wrong and make some changes, it will affect your mate's thoughts and feelings, and perhaps even behavior.

Maybe you think you're not doing anything wrong. But even if your mate is 99 percent responsible for all the problems of the marriage, you can still look at the 1 percent that's your responsibility. It's amazing what can be accomplished by changing even 1 percent of your behavior.

And, as you progress in counseling and your spouse begins to see changes, she or he may decide to give it a try as well. This is even more likely to happen if we don't hammer the subject to death. Have you ever been around a person who is so excited about a new religion or program that he drives you away? You cringe when you see him approaching, knowing you're going to get another sales pitch about why you should switch churches or go to a health-food lecture or take a personal-growth seminar. The harder he tries to get you to go, the more determined you are to resist.

On the other hand, if you see an unhappy person begin to get happier, you wonder why. You watch to see if it will continue. If it does, you begin to want some of whatever it is that seems so effective.

By going alone to a counselor you're telling your mate, in effect, "I'm really unhappy. I can't seem to resolve my problems, so I'm going for help. I'd love to have you join me, but I'm going even if you don't. If you ever want to come along, you're welcome . . . and I'll be delighted!"

When You've Done All You Can

What if you're living in an impossible situation that you can't cope with anymore, but your mate refuses to discuss it, get help, or make any changes? How long must you live that way?

Most of us need help in that situation. If not a counselor (which would be my first recommendation), then a good friend, family member, or someone at your church or synagogue. Sometimes you're so close to a situation you lose perspective and become frozen—miserable and unable to move in any productive kind of way.

A typical example is the husband or wife of an alcoholic or drug addict. It becomes a rotten way to live, affecting every aspect of the family. The problem touches all the lives in a sad, destructive way, sometimes continuing for years because no one knows quite what to do.

I can't say enough good things about Al-Anon, an organization designed just for that situation. If you go, you'll learn how to handle everything. You hear other people share their experiences and it's like hearing your own family talking. You may realize for the first time you're not alone—millions of people

> Sometimes you're so close to a situation you lose perspective and become frozen— miserable and unable to move in any productive kind of way.

have been in the same boat. And now you have their accumulated experience and wisdom to draw from. Many people are reluctant to go for fear of being seen and recognized, but everyone there has someone in their lives who's into some addictive behavior. You'll probably make some friends there who will become close to you, friends you'll treasure. Look for Al-Anon in your *Yellow Pages* under "Alcoholism Treatment."

You don't have to live in a wretched situation. But you may need help to discover some of the options to consider for finding relief.

No matter what problem you have with a mate, the advice is the same. Get some outside help. No one has to put up with abuse—verbal, physical, or sexual. Nor should our children have to endure it.

Commitment to marriage does not mean we have to stay stuck in a rotten situation, but we may need help in getting ourselves unstuck.

The "D" Word

Some people decide to separate. They've talked themselves blue, trying to get a spouse to acknowledge a problem, but it seems to fall on deaf ears. Finally they know they're licked, and they tell their partners something like this:

"I'm defeated. I've hurt so much for so long, and I haven't been able to get any help from you in dealing with our problems. I can't do it alone. I'm too discouraged to keep trying because I know you don't think there's a problem, and I can't change you. I need to take care of myself, though. I'm going to start looking for an apartment."

If you say it, mean it. Don't use it as manipulation. Do it only when you've tried every avenue for improving the situation and come to nothing but dead ends.

Sadly, a disinterested mate often sits up and takes notice when it's too late. I wish I had a nickel for every marriage I've seen in that last fatal stage, when either the wife or the husband is throwing in the towel. Usually the more submissive party has swallowed a lot of anger for some years and now has suddenly become assertive and won't take any more.

Too many times the marriage could have been saved if it had been attended to earlier. If your partner is telling you there's a problem in the marriage, please *believe* it! If one person has a problem, both people have a problem, and it needs to be addressed.

Another strong conviction I have about leaving a marriage is this: Falling in love with another person is the wrong reason for leaving. In that euphoric state, we're back to the insanity we felt for our prince or princess in the beginning. I own a marble paperweight on which is printed, "A person in love is a very poor judge of character." I might add that a person in love is a poor judge of almost everything, so that's certainly not the right time to get a divorce.

> When you leave a partner for his imperfections and marry another, you have to cope with different imperfections. You could go through a lot of partners that way.

One comment I hear from troubled spouses is, "You know, as I've thought about it over the years, I think I could have made my first marriage work if I'd been willing to work at it. The other grass is always greener."

When you leave a partner for his imperfections and marry another, you have to cope with different imperfections. You could go through a lot of partners that way. It's easier to keep working on the one you've got.

Nevertheless, I do recognize the fact that some marriages were a mistake in the first place. I sometimes heave a great sigh of relief when the couples agree to end it. It's not so hard to watch a divorce when both people want out.

It's difficult when only one does. The person who's left really needs help to deal with all the grief he or she will be going through—the same stages of grief you go through in losing someone to death (denial, bargaining, anger, depression, and finally acceptance).

The person leaving generally has been planning to exit for some time and sees the step as a positive one, one that's necessary to relieve pain. The other faces a tremendous shock, filled with profound hurt and anger. That person needs a lot of encouragement in order to move toward acceptance.

I had a client named Bill who was in just that position.

He was so devastated by the loss of his marriage that he became depressed and finally suicidal. One evening he swallowed a lot of pills and lay down to die.

"As I was beginning to feel a numbness throughout my body, I got frightened," he recounted later. "I realized I didn't want to give up this life. Suddenly I knew how much I wanted to live, and I was so numb and fuzzy, I could hardly pick up the phone. I did manage to, by the grace of God, and somehow got an operator who sent out the paramedics." He was rushed to the hospital and released a few days later.

When I saw him next, he was a different man. The depression was gone and he was obviously ready to live life again. In those moments of near-death, he'd turned a corner and decided to embrace the future positively. From then on our therapy was easy.

At the end of his last session he said, "If there's ever anyone you think I could help, please call me. I think I could understand someone who feels the way I felt, and I'd be glad to do whatever I could."

Several months later I met Anne, a sad, sweet lady who was struggling with her own depression. We worked together for a while and I told her about Bill who had offered a kind ear to anyone in that position. She was dubious, but decided to meet him for coffee.

A year later they invited me to their wedding. Every now and then when I run into them, they're still holding hands. Those two give me goose bumps, they're so happy, and they're proof that life can be even happier than it was before. Being left by a spouse is not the end of the world.

People have an amazing ability to adjust. We never *have* to stay unhappy.

Still, many divorces I've seen wouldn't have happened if the people involved knew a little more about improving marriage instead of junking it. Sometimes I think it's almost contagious; seeing friends divorce each other makes it seem more and more acceptable. It becomes simpler to quit working on the discouraging relationship and opt for what appears to be a better solution: just get out.

We've gotten used to fast foods, whipping into drive-thru lanes for a quick-fix of burger, fries, and drink in less than two minutes. But we all know that a sumptuous dinner tastes a lot better, lasts longer, and is ever so much more nutritious. It takes longer to fix and to eat, but the overall reward is one most of us would choose any day over a quickie burger.

> Many divorces I've seen wouldn't have happened if the people involved knew a little more about improving marriage instead of junking it.

A lifetime marriage on which we spend time and energy is going to be the most satisfying, sumptuous feast we could want, well worth the work it takes.

I'm picturing two friends of ours who are in their golden years. Retired and enjoying life thoroughly, they had us over for dinner one night and were proudly showing us around their home. We admired a fireplace, and the woman said, "We love it. We use it a lot, all winter. Sometimes we make love right here on the rug in the firelight," and they looked fondly at each other.

I was moved at the love I saw in their eyes and hoped I would feel as loving toward Larry when we are their age.

I know I can, but not unless I keep trying. There are still those times when I don't feel any noticeable love for him; in fact, I don't even much *like* him. I've even thought occasionally, "I don't want to put up with this anymore. Maybe I oughta get me a little townhouse and live there all by myself."

But I know, too, it's a temporary stage, and I'll get over it. Sometimes I've prayed, "Help me love him more." And sometimes even, "Help me *want* to love him more," when I've been really put off.

It no longer alarms me when I feel that hostility, because I always end up loving him again. I reflect on those times and liken my attitude to a sulky kid who's all bent out of shape because the cookies are gone.

I can dig my heels into the ground and wallow in self-pity if I want. Or complain to all the neighbors that the cookie jar is bare. I

> Most of us married for the wrong reasons: romantic excitement, sexual chemistry, and someone to take care of us, filling our every need. But if we keep working at it, we'll probably end up being married for the *right* reasons.

might even choose to lash out at someone in the house who I think should provide me with my cookie supply.

But one of the advantages of being grown up is resourcefulness in providing my own cookies. I can bake them or buy them, but it's up to me to keep my supply replenished.

If I'm unhappy, I am the one to see about it. When I get sufficiently miserable with my life I can say, "I don't have to put up with this kind of behavior from myself anymore," and set about finding solutions.

Most of us married for the wrong reasons: romantic excitement, sexual chemistry, and someone to take care of us, filling our every need. But if we keep working at it, we'll probably end up being married for the *right* reasons.

Having someone in life who knows us better than anyone else. Someone who tolerates our bad behavior in exchange for the right to exhibit some as well. Someone we can nurture and care about, but not feel responsible for. A person to hug. A driver to provide the sound of a familiar car coming home. A partner to share both the pleasure and the pain of raising children. And the special pride of hearing a grandchild begin to talk. Not a perfect person who might intimidate us by contrast, but an ordinary velveteen-rabbit-type person who grows more loveable with all the years of pummeling that life dishes out. A sharer of thousands of memories and inside jokes that guarantee a smile. Eyes to meet across a room that understand, "I want to go home." A friend to cry with. Someone with whom to make love on the rug by the fireplace when we're old. Tenderly.

I Wish You Love

People often ask, "Uh . . . how does Larry feel about your honesty in these books? I mean, you're pretty open, don't you think?"

I am. And so is Larry. Over the years we've realized we're really much like everybody else, so there's not a lot to hide. Still, I would not have let a chapter go to press without his approval. He read each one as I finished it and made encouraging comments all along the way. He's also carted hundreds of boxes of books to seminars and post offices. I cherish his constant support!

Laurie takes my hastily typed copy and edits it skillfully, bringing clarity and order to my jumbled first draft. I couldn't produce a book without her advice, professional expertise, and enthusiasm.

Lisa shoots great pictures for the back covers of some of my books. Also, she and I trade theories and thoughts by the hour, and much of my writing is inspired by her fresh, creative thinking.

Lindsay and Lyle have yet to read one of my books. "We know everything you have to say, Mom," they explain. But they compliment my pork chops and dumplings.

A Gift For You

I give newlyweds a message in the form of a poem I wrote about the importance of communication. I enclose this poem in a box with two silver goblets, an unusual wedding gift. You have my permission to copy the poem if you'd like to encourage conversation, too.

Dear   and
These goblets are magic, as you will attest
When you've used them and found that they bring out the best
Of the love that's between you: a wonderful thing!
It's precious and endless, like your wedding ring.
Here's how they work: When you two have a fight,
Whether it's small or lasts long in the night,
Either can get out the goblets and pour
Some beverage for drinking "an end to the war."
Just offer the goblet, a gesture of peace.
The message implies, "Let's let anger cease."

"To us!" you both say as you toast one another.
You sip and you listen and talk to each other.
Often the magic works quickly and well,
And soon the solution is clear as a bell.
But when the cup's empty, if things aren't okay,
Just pour a bit more and keep chatting away.
If you talk long enough in a kind, gentle way,
The problem may solve itself that very day.
The magic continues as long as you each
Converse with respect. Understanding you'll reach.
But if, in the course of sipping and talking,
Either starts crying or shouting or walking,
Then stop for a while. It might be the best
To bring it up later when you've had a rest.
You can drink from them anytime, happy or sad,
But the magic is strongest when feelings are bad.
With enough conversation these goblets assure
That your life will be happy. Your love will endure!

—Lee Schnebly

Recommended
Reading

Baron, Renee, and Elizabeth Wagele. *Are You My Type, Am I Yours?*
San Francisco: Harper San Francisco, 1995.

_____. *The Enneagram Made Easy: Discover the 9 Types of People.* San
Francisco: Harper San Francisco, 1994.

Carnes, Patrick. *Out of the Shadows: Understanding Sexual Addiction.*
Center City, Minn.: Hazelden Information Education, 1992.

Diets, Bob. *Life After Loss.* Tucson, Ariz.: Fisher Books, 2000.

Dinkmeyer, Don, and Gary McKay. *The Parent's Handbook:
Systematic Training for Effective Parenting.* Circle Pines, Minn.:
American Guidance Service, 1997.

Dobson, James. *Love Must Be Tough: Proven Help for Families in
Crisis.* Nashville, Tenn.: Word Books, 1996.

_____. *What Wives Wish Their Husbands Knew about Women.*
Wheaton, Ill.: Tyndale House, 1988.

Dyer, Wayne. *Your Erroneous Zones.* New York: Harper, 1999.

Ellis, Albert, and Robert Harper. *A New Guide To Rational Living.*
North Hollywood: Wilshire Book Co., 1998.

Glasser, William. *Positive Addiction.* New York: HarperCollins, 1985.

Gray, John. *Men Are from Mars, Women Are from Venus.* New York:
HarperCollins, 1992.

_____. *Practical Miracles for Mars and Venus.* New York: HarperCollins, 2000.

Guhl, Beverly, and Don Fontenelle. *Purrfect Parenting.* Tucson, Ariz.: Fisher Books, 2000.

Hendrix, Harville. *Getting the Love You Want.* New York: Harper Perennial, 1990.

Jampolsky, Gerald. *Love Is Letting Go of Fear.* Berkeley, Calif.: Celestial Arts, 1988.

Leman, Kevin. *Making Children Mind Without Losing Yours.* Grand Rapids, Mich.: Fleming H. Revell Co., 2000.

_____. *Sex Begins in the Kitchen.* Grand Rapids, Mich.: Fleming H. Revell Co., 2000.

Lerner, Harriet. *The Dance of Anger.* New York: HarperCollins, 1997.

_____. *The Dance of Intimacy.* New York: HarperCollins, 1990.

McGraw, Philip. *Relationship Rescue.* New York: Hyperion, 2000.

Powell, John. *The Secret of Staying in Love.* Allen, Tex.: Thomas More Press, 1995.

Schnebly, Lee. *Do-It-Yourself Happiness.* Tucson, Ariz.: Fisher Books, 1988.

_____. *Nurturing Yourself and Others.* Tucson, Ariz.: Fisher Books, 2000.

Schneider, Jennifer. *Back From Betrayal.* New York: HarperCollins, 1990.

Smalley, Gary. *For Better or for Best.* Grand Rapids, Mich.: Zondervan Publishing, 1996.

_____. *If Only He Knew.* Grand Rapids, Mich.: Zondervan Publishing, 1996.

Smalley, Gary, and John Trent. *The Language of Love.* New York: Pocket Books, 1995.

Index

About the Author

Lee Schnebly is a certified mental-health counselor in Tucson, Arizona. She specializes in marriage, family, and individual counseling. Her warm, lighthearted style makes her a popular author and speaker. Her speeches and books make you feel refreshed and uplifted.

Lee's prior books are *Nurturing Yourself and Others* and *Do-It-Yourself Happiness*. In them you will find additional encouragement and discover what makes you happy. Lee invites you to enjoy life to the fullest!